A Tour of C++

The C++ In-Depth Series
BJARNE STROUSTRUP, Editor

"I have made this letter longer than usual, because I lack the time to make it short."
— Blaise Pascal

The C++ In-Depth Series is a collection of concise and focused books providing real-world programmers with reliable information about the C++ programming language. Selected by the designer and original implementer of C++, Bjarne Stroustrup, and written by experts in the field, each book in this series presents either a single topic, at a technical level appropriate to that topic, or a fast-paced overview, for a quick understanding of broader language features. Its practical approach, in either case, is designed to lift professionals (and aspiring professionals) to the next level of programming skill or knowledge.

These short books are meant to be read and referenced without the distraction of unrelated material. As C++ matures, it becomes increasingly important to be able to separate essential information from hype and glitz, and to find the deep content and practical guidance needed for continued development. The C++ In-Depth Series provides the background, tools, concepts, techniques, and new approaches that can enable this development, and thereby give readers a valuable, critical edge.

A Tour of C++

Bjarne Stroustrup

✦✦Addison-Wesley

Upper Saddle River, NJ • Boston • Indianapolis • San Francisco
New York • Toronto • Montreal • London • Munich • Paris • Madrid
Capetown • Sydney • Tokyo • Singapore • Mexico City

Many of the designations used by manufacturers and sellers to distinguish their products are claimed as trademarks. Where those designations appear in this book, and the publisher was aware of a trademark claim, the designations have been printed with initial capital letters or in all capitals.

The author and publisher have taken care in the preparation of this book, but make no expressed or implied warranty of any kind and assume no responsibility for errors or omissions. No liability is assumed for incidental or consequential damages in connection with or arising out of the use of the information or programs contained herein.

The publisher offers excellent discounts on this book when ordered in quantity for bulk purchases or special sales, which may include electronic versions and/or custom covers and content particular to your business, training goals, marketing focus, and branding interests. For more information, please contact:

U.S. Corporate and Government Sales
(800) 382-3419
corpsales@pearsontechgroup.com

For sales outside the United States, please contact:
International Sales
international@pearsoned.com

Visit us on the Web: informit.com/aw

Library of Congress Cataloging-in-Publication Data

Stroustrup, Bjarne.
    A Tour of C++ / Bjarne Stroustrup.
        pages cm
    Includes bibliographical references and index.
    ISBN 978-0-321-958310 (pbk. : alk. paper)—ISBN 0-321-958314 (pbk. : alk. paper)
    1. C++ (Computer programming language) I. Title.

QA76.73.C153 S77 2013
005.13′3—dc23   2013002159

This book was typeset in Times and Helvetica by the author.

ISBN-13: 978-0-321-958310
ISBN-10:   0-321-958314
Text printed in the United States on recycled paper at Edwards Brothers Malloy in Ann Arbor, Michigan.
Fourth printing, July 2015

Contents

Preface

C++ feels like a new language. That is, I can express my ideas more clearly, more simply, and more directly in C++11 than I could in C++98. Furthermore, the resulting programs are better checked by the compiler and run faster.

Like other modern languages, C++ is large and there are a large number of libraries needed for effective use. This thin book aims to give an experienced programmer an idea of what constitutes modern C++. It covers most major language features and the major standard-library components. This book can be read in just a few hours but, obviously, there is much more to writing good C++ than can be learned in a day. However, the aim here is not mastery, but to give an overview, to give key examples, and to help a programmer get started. For mastery, consider my *The C++ Programming Language, Fourth Edition* (TC++PL4) [Stroustrup,2013]. In fact, this book is an extended version of the material that constitutes Chapters 2-5 of TC++PL4, also entitled *A Tour of C++*. I have added extensions and improvements to make this book reasonably self-contained. The structure of this tour follows that of TC++PL4, so it is easy to find supplementary material. Similarly, the exercises for TC++PL4 that are available on my Web site (www.stroustrup.com) can be used to support this tour.

The assumption is that you have programmed before. If not, please consider reading a textbook, such as *Programming: Principles and Practice Using C++* [Stroustrup,2009], before continuing here. Even if you have programmed before, the language you used or the applications you wrote may be very different from the style of C++ presented here.

As an analogy, think of a short sightseeing tour of a city, such as Copenhagen or New York. In just a few hours, you are given a quick peek at the major attractions, told a few background stories, and usually given some suggestions about what to see next. You do *not* know the city after such a tour. You do *not* understand all you have seen and heard. You do *not* know how to navigate the formal and informal rules that govern life in the city. To really know a city, you have to live in it, often for years. However, with a bit of luck, you will have gained a bit of an overview, a notion of what is special about the city, and ideas of what might be of interest to you. After the tour, the real exploration can begin.

This tour presents the major C++ language features as they support programming styles, such as object-oriented and generic programming. It does not attempt to provide a detailed, reference-manual, feature-by-feature view of the language. Similarly, it presents the standard libraries in terms of examples, rather than exhaustively. It does not describe libraries beyond those defined by the ISO standard. The reader can search out supporting material as needed. [Stroustrup,2009] and [Stroustrup,2013] are examples of such material, but there is an enormous amount of material (of varying quality) available on the Web. For example, when I mention a standard library function or class, its definition can easily be looked up, and by examining the documentation of its header (also easily accessible on the Web), many related facilities can be found.

This tour presents C++ as an integrated whole, rather than as a layer cake. Consequently, it does not identify language features as present in C, part of C++98, or new in C++11. Such information can be found in Chapter 14 (History and Compatibility).

Acknowledgments

Much of the material presented here is borrowed from TC++PL4 [Stroustrup,2013], so thanks to all who helped completing that book. Also, thanks to my editor at Addison-Wesley, Peter Gordon, who first suggested that the four Tour chapters from TC++PL4 might be expanded into a reasonably self-contained and consistent publication of their own.

College Station, Texas   *Bjarne Stroustrup*

1

The Basics

The first thing we do, let's
kill all the language lawyers.
– Henry VI, Part II

- Introduction
- Programs
- Hello, World!
- Functions
- Types, Variables, and Arithmetic
- Scope and Lifetime
- Constants
- Pointers, Arrays, and References
- Tests
- Advice

1.1 Introduction

This chapter informally presents the notation of C++, C++'s model of memory and computation, and the basic mechanisms for organizing code into a program. These are the language facilities supporting the styles most often seen in C and sometimes called *procedural programming*.

1.2 Programs

C++ is a compiled language. For a program to run, its source text has to be processed by a compiler, producing object files, which are combined by a linker yielding an executable program. A C++ program typically consists of many source code files (usually simply called *source files*).

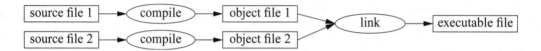

An executable program is created for a specific hardware/system combination; it is not portable, say, from a Mac to a Windows PC. When we talk about portability of C++ programs, we usually mean portability of source code; that is, the source code can be successfully compiled and run on a variety of systems.

The ISO C++ standard defines two kinds of entities:
- *Core language features*, such as built-in types (e.g., **char** and **int**) and loops (e.g., **for**-statements and **while**-statements)
- *Standard-library components*, such as containers (e.g., **vector** and **map**) and I/O operations (e.g., **<<** and **getline()**)

The standard-library components are perfectly ordinary C++ code provided by every C++ implementation. That is, the C++ standard library can be implemented in C++ itself (and is with very minor uses of machine code for things such as thread context switching). This implies that C++ is sufficiently expressive and efficient for the most demanding systems programming tasks.

C++ is a statically typed language. That is, the type of every entity (e.g., object, value, name, and expression) must be known to the compiler at its point of use. The type of an object determines the set of operations applicable to it.

1.3 Hello, World!

The minimal C++ program is

```
int main() { }        // the minimal C++ program
```

This defines a function called **main**, which takes no arguments and does nothing.

Curly braces, **{ }**, express grouping in C++. Here, they indicate the start and end of the function body. The double slash, **//**, begins a comment that extends to the end of the line. A comment is for the human reader; the compiler ignores comments.

Every C++ program must have exactly one global function named **main()**. The program starts by executing that function. The **int** integer value returned by **main()**, if any, is the program's return value to "the system." If no value is returned, the system will receive a value indicating successful completion. A nonzero value from **main()** indicates failure. Not every operating system and execution environment make use of that return value: Linux/Unix-based environments often do, but Windows-based environments rarely do.

Typically, a program produces some output. Here is a program that writes **Hello, World!**:

```
#include <iostream>

int main()
{
    std::cout << "Hello, World!\n";
}
```

The line #include <iostream> instructs the compiler to *include* the declarations of the standard stream I/O facilities as found in iostream. Without these declarations, the expression

    std::cout << "Hello, World!\n"

would make no sense. The operator << ("put to") writes its second argument onto its first. In this case, the string literal "Hello, World!\n" is written onto the standard output stream std::cout. A string literal is a sequence of characters surrounded by double quotes. In a string literal, the backslash character \ followed by another character denotes a single "special character." In this case, \n is the newline character, so that the characters written are Hello, World! followed by a newline.

The std:: specifies that the name cout is to be found in the standard-library namespace (§3.3). I usually leave out the std:: when discussing standard features; §3.3 shows how to make names from a namespace visible without explicit qualification.

Essentially all executable code is placed in functions and called directly or indirectly from main(). For example:

```cpp
#include <iostream>          // include ("import") the declarations for the I/O stream library

using namespace std;         // make names from std visible without std:: (§3.3)

double square(double x)      // square a double precision floating-point number
{
    return x*x;
}

void print_square(double x)
{
    cout << "the square of " << x << " is " << square(x) << "\n";
}

int main()
{
    print_square(1.234);     // print: the square of 1.234 is 1.52276
}
```

A "return type" void indicates that a function does not return a value.

1.4 Functions

The main way of getting something done in a C++ program is to call a function to do it. Defining a function is the way you specify how an operation is to be done. A function cannot be called unless it has been previously declared.

A function declaration gives the name of the function, the type of the value returned (if any), and the number and types of the arguments that must be supplied in a call. For example:

```cpp
Elem* next_elem();          // no argument; return a pointer to Elem (an Elem*)
void exit(int);             // int argument; return nothing
double sqrt(double);        // double argument; return a double
```

In a function declaration, the return type comes before the name of the function and the argument types after the name enclosed in parentheses.

The semantics of argument passing are identical to the semantics of copy initialization. That is, argument types are checked and implicit argument type conversion takes place when necessary (§1.5). For example:

```
double s2 = sqrt(2);            // call sqrt() with the argument double{2}
double s3 = sqrt("three");      // error: sqrt() requires an argument of type double
```

The value of such compile-time checking and type conversion should not be underestimated.

A function declaration may contain argument names. This can be a help to the reader of a program, but unless the declaration is also a function definition, the compiler simply ignores such names. For example:

```
double sqrt(double d);    // return the square root of d
double square(double);    // return the square of the argument
```

The type of a function consists of the return type and the argument types. For class member functions (§2.3, §4.2.1), the name of the class is also part of the function type. For example:

```
double get(const vector<double>& vec, int index);    // type: double(const vector<double>&,int)
char& String::operator[](int index);                 // type: char& String::(int)
```

We want our code to be comprehensible, because that is the first step on the way to maintainability. The first step to comprehensibility is to break computational tasks into comprehensible chunks (represented as functions and classes) and name those. Such functions then provide the basic vocabulary of computation, just as the types (built-in and user-defined) provide the basic vocabulary of data. The C++ standard algorithms (e.g., **find**, **sort**, and **iota**) provide a good start (Chapter 10). Next, we can compose functions representing common or specialized tasks into larger computations.

The number of errors in code correlates strongly with the amount of code and the complexity of the code. Both problems can be addressed by using more and shorter functions. Using a function to do a specific task often saves us from writing a specific piece of code in the middle of other code; making it a function forces us to name the activity and document its dependencies.

If two functions are defined with the same name, but with different argument types, the compiler will choose the most appropriate function to invoke for each call. For example:

```
void print(int);       // takes an integer argument
void print(double);    // takes a floating-point argument
void print(string);    // takes a string argument

void user()
{
    print(42);                   // calls print(int)
    print(9.65);                 // calls print(double)
    print("D is for Digital");   // calls print(string)
}
```

If two alternative functions could be called, but neither is better than the other, the call is deemed ambiguous and the compiler gives an error. For example:

```
void print(int,double);
void print(double,int);

void user2()
{
    print(0,0);        // error: ambiguous
}
```

This is known as function overloading and is one of the essential parts of generic programming (§5.4). When a function is overloaded, each function of the same name should implement the same semantics. The print() functions are an example of this; each print() prints its argument.

1.5 Types, Variables, and Arithmetic

Every name and every expression has a type that determines the operations that may be performed on it. For example, the declaration

```
int inch;
```

specifies that inch is of type int; that is, inch is an integer variable.

A *declaration* is a statement that introduces a name into the program. It specifies a type for the named entity:

- A *type* defines a set of possible values and a set of operations (for an object).
- An *object* is some memory that holds a value of some type.
- A *value* is a set of bits interpreted according to a type.
- A *variable* is a named object.

C++ offers a variety of fundamental types. For example:

```
bool          // Boolean, possible values are true and false
char          // character, for example, 'a', 'z', and '9'
int           // integer, for example, -273, 42, and 1066
double        // double-precision floating-point number, for example, -273.15, 3.14, and 299793.0
unsigned      // non-negative integer, for example, 0, 1, and 999
```

Each fundamental type corresponds directly to hardware facilities and has a fixed size that determines the range of values that can be stored in it:

A char variable is of the natural size to hold a character on a given machine (typically an 8-bit byte), and the sizes of other types are quoted in multiples of the size of a char. The size of a type is implementation-defined (i.e., it can vary among different machines) and can be obtained by the sizeof operator; for example, sizeof(char) equals 1 and sizeof(int) is often 4.

The arithmetic operators can be used for appropriate combinations of these types:

```
x+y        // plus
+x         // unary plus
x−y        // minus
−x         // unary minus
x*y        // multiply
x/y        // divide
x%y        // remainder (modulus) for integers
```

So can the comparison operators:

```
x==y       // equal
x!=y       // not equal
x<y        // less than
x>y        // greater than
x<=y       // less than or equal
x>=y       // greater than or equal
```

Furthermore, logical operators are provided:

```
x&y        // bitwise and
x|y        // bitwise or
x^y        // bitwise exclusive or
~x         // bitwise complement
x&&y       // logical and
x||y       // logical or
```

A bitwise logical operator yields a result of the operand type for which the operation has been performed on each bit. The logical operators && and || simply return true or false depending on the values of their operands.

In assignments and in arithmetic operations, C++ performs all meaningful conversions between the basic types so that they can be mixed freely:

```
void some_function()       // function that doesn't return a value
{
     double d = 2.2;        // initialize floating-point number
     int i = 7;             // initialize integer
     d = d+i;               // assign sum to d
     i = d*i;               // assign product to i (truncating the double d*i to an int)
}
```

The conversions used in expressions are called *the usual arithmetic conversions* and aim to ensure that expressions are computed at the highest precision of its operands. For example, an addition of a double and an int is calculated using double-precision floating-point arithmetic.

Note that = is the assignment operator and == tests equality.

C++ offers a variety of notations for expressing initialization, such as the = used above, and a universal form based on curly-brace-delimited initializer lists:

```
double d1 = 2.3;           // initialize d1 to 2.3
double d2 {2.3};           // initialize d2 to 2.3
```

```
complex<double> z = 1;              // a complex number with double-precision floating-point scalars
complex<double> z2 {d1,d2};
complex<double> z3 = {1,2};         // the = is optional with { ... }

vector<int> v {1,2,3,4,5,6};        // a vector of ints
```

The = form is traditional and dates back to C, but if in doubt, use the general {}-list form. If nothing else, it saves you from conversions that lose information:

```
int i1 = 7.8;          // i1 becomes 7 (surprise?)
int i2 {7.8};          // error: floating-point to integer conversion
int i3 = {7.8};        // error: floating-point to integer conversion (the = is redundant)
```

Unfortunately, conversions that lose information, *narrowing conversions*, such as **double** to **int** and **int** to **char** are allowed and implicitly applied. The problems caused by implicit narrowing conversions is a price paid for C compatibility (§14.3).

A constant (§1.7) cannot be left uninitialized and a variable should only be left uninitialized in extremely rare circumstances. Don't introduce a name until you have a suitable value for it. User-defined types (such as **string**, **vector**, **Matrix**, **Motor_controller**, and **Orc_warrior**) can be defined to be implicitly initialized (§4.2.1).

When defining a variable, you don't actually need to state its type explicitly when it can be deduced from the initializer:

```
auto b = true;         // a bool
auto ch = 'x';         // a char
auto i = 123;          // an int
auto d = 1.2;          // a double
auto z = sqrt(y);      // z has the type of whatever sqrt(y) returns
```

With **auto**, we use the = because there is no potentially troublesome type conversion involved.

We use **auto** where we don't have a specific reason to mention the type explicitly. "Specific reasons" include:

- The definition is in a large scope where we want to make the type clearly visible to readers of our code.
- We want to be explicit about a variable's range or precision (e.g., **double** rather than **float**).

Using **auto**, we avoid redundancy and writing long type names. This is especially important in generic programming where the exact type of an object can be hard for the programmer to know and the type names can be quite long (§10.2).

In addition to the conventional arithmetic and logical operators, C++ offers more specific operations for modifying a variable:

```
x+=y        // x = x+y
++x         // increment: x = x+1
x−=y        // x = x-y
−−x         // decrement: x = x-1
x*=y        // scaling: x = x*y
x/=y        // scaling: x = x/y
x%=y        // x = x%y
```

These operators are concise, convenient, and very frequently used.

1.6 Scope and Lifetime

A declaration introduces its name into a scope:

- *Local scope*: A name declared in a function (§1.4) or lambda (§5.5) is called a *local name*. Its scope extends from its point of declaration to the end of the block in which its declaration occurs. A *block* is delimited by a { } pair. Function argument names are considered local names.
- *Class scope*: A name is called a *member name* (or a *class member name*) if it is defined in a class (§2.2, §2.3, Chapter 4), outside any function (§1.4), lambda (§5.5), or **enum class** (§2.5). Its scope extends from the opening { of its enclosing declaration to the end of that declaration.
- *Namespace scope*: A name is called a *namespace member name* if it is defined in a namespace (§3.3) outside any function, lambda (§5.5), class (§2.2, §2.3, Chapter 4), or **enum class** (§2.5). Its scope extends from the point of declaration to the end of its namespace.

A name not declared inside any other construct is called a *global name* and is said to be in the *global namespace*.

In addition, we can have objects without names, such as temporaries and objects created using **new** (§4.2.2). For example:

```
vector<int> vec;        // vec is global (a global vector of integers)

struct Record {
    string name;        // name is a member (a string member)
    // ...
};

void fct(int arg)       // fct is global (a global function)
                        // arg is local (an integer argument)
{
    string motto {"Who dares wins"};   // motto is local
    auto p = new Record{"Hume"};       // p points to an unnamed Record (created by new)
    // ...
}
```

An object must be constructed (initialized) before it is used and will be destroyed at the end of its scope. For a namespace object the point of destruction is the end of the program. For a member, the point of destruction is determined by the point of destruction of the object of which it is a member. An object created by **new** "lives" until destroyed by **delete** (§4.2.2).

1.7 Constants

C++ supports two notions of immutability:

- **const**: meaning roughly "I promise not to change this value." This is used primarily to specify interfaces, so that data can be passed to functions without fear of it being modified. The compiler enforces the promise made by **const**.

- **constexpr**: meaning roughly "to be evaluated at compile time." This is used primarily to specify constants, to allow placement of data in read-only memory (where it is unlikely to be corrupted) and for performance.

For example:

```
const int dmv = 17;                    // dmv is a named constant
int var = 17;                          // var is not a constant

constexpr double max1 = 1.4*square(dmv);   // OK if square(17) is a constant expression
constexpr double max2 = 1.4*square(var);   // error: var is not a constant expression
const double max3 = 1.4*square(var);       // OK, may be evaluated at run time

double sum(const vector<double>&);     // sum will not modify its argument (§1.8)
vector<double> v {1.2, 3.4, 4.5};      // v is not a constant
const double s1 = sum(v);              // OK: evaluated at run time
constexpr double s2 = sum(v);          // error: sum(v) not constant expression
```

For a function to be usable in a *constant expression*, that is, in an expression that will be evaluated by the compiler, it must be defined **constexpr**. For example:

```
constexpr double square(double x) { return x*x; }
```

To be **constexpr**, a function must be rather simple: just a **return**-statement computing a value. A **constexpr** function can be used for non-constant arguments, but when that is done the result is not a constant expression. We allow a **constexpr** function to be called with non-constant-expression arguments in contexts that do not require constant expressions, so that we don't have to define essentially the same function twice: once for constant expressions and once for variables.

In a few places, constant expressions are required by language rules (e.g., array bounds (§1.8), case labels (§1.9), template value arguments (§5.2), and constants declared using **constexpr**). In other cases, compile-time evaluation is important for performance. Independently of performance issues, the notion of immutability (of an object with an unchangeable state) is an important design concern.

1.8 Pointers, Arrays, and References

An array of elements of type **char** can be declared like this:

```
char v[6];          // array of 6 characters
```

Similarly, a pointer can be declared like this:

```
char* p;            // pointer to character
```

In declarations, [ ] means "array of" and * means "pointer to." All arrays have 0 as their lower bound, so v has six elements, v[0] to v[5]. The size of an array must be a constant expression (§1.7). A pointer variable can hold the address of an object of the appropriate type:

```
char* p = &v[3];    // p points to v's fourth element
char x = *p;        // *p is the object that p points to
```

In an expression, prefix unary * means "contents of" and prefix unary & means "address of." We can represent the result of that initialized definition graphically:

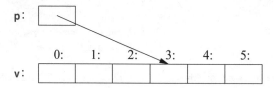

Consider copying ten elements from one array to another:

```
void copy_fct()
{
    int v1[10] = {0,1,2,3,4,5,6,7,8,9};
    int v2[10];                 // to become a copy of v1

    for (auto i=0; i!=10; ++i)  // copy elements
        v2[i]=v1[i];
    // ...
}
```

This for-statement can be read as "set i to zero; while i is not 10, copy the ith element and increment i." When applied to an integer variable, the increment operator, ++, simply adds 1. C++ also offers a simpler for-statement, called a range-for-statement, for loops that traverse a sequence in the simplest way:

```
void print()
{
    int v[] = {0,1,2,3,4,5,6,7,8,9};

    for (auto x : v)            // for each x in v
        cout << x << '\n';

    for (auto x : {10,21,32,43,54,65})
        cout << x << '\n';
    // ...
}
```

The first range-for-statement can be read as "for every element of v, from the first to the last, place a copy in x and print it." Note that we don't have to specify an array bound when we initialize it with a list. The range-for-statement can be used for any sequence of elements (§10.1).

If we didn't want to copy the values from v into the variable x, but rather just have x refer to an element, we could write:

```
void increment()
{
    int v[] = {0,1,2,3,4,5,6,7,8,9};
```

```
        for (auto& x : v)
            ++x;
    // ...
}
```

In a declaration, the unary suffix **&** means "reference to." A reference is similar to a pointer, except that you don't need to use a prefix * to access the value referred to by the reference. Also, a reference cannot be made to refer to a different object after its initialization.

References are particularly useful for specifying function arguments. For example:

```
void sort(vector<double>& v);        // sort v
```

By using a reference, we ensure that for a call **sort(my_vec)**, we do not copy **my_vec** and that it really is **my_vec** that is sorted and not a copy of it.

When we don't want to modify an argument, but still don't want the cost of copying, we use a **const** reference. For example:

```
double sum(const vector<double>&)
```

Functions taking **const** references are very common.

When used in declarations, operators (such as **&**, *, and **[ ]**) are called *declarator operators*:

```
T a[n];     // T[n]: array of n Ts
T* p;       // T*: pointer to T
T& r;       // T&: reference to T
T f(A);     // T(A): function taking an argument of type A returning a result of type T
```

We try to ensure that a pointer always points to an object, so that dereferencing it is valid. When we don't have an object to point to or if we need to represent the notion of "no object available" (e.g., for an end of a list), we give the pointer the value **nullptr** ("the null pointer"). There is only one **nullptr** shared by all pointer types:

```
double* pd = nullptr;
Link<Record>* lst = nullptr;     // pointer to a Link to a Record
int x = nullptr;                 // error: nullptr is a pointer not an integer
```

It is often wise to check that a pointer argument that is supposed to point to something, actually points to something:

```
int count_x(char* p, char x)
    // count the number of occurrences of x in p[]
    // p is assumed to point to a zero-terminated array of char (or to nothing)
{
    if (p==nullptr) return 0;
    int count = 0;
    for (; *p!=0; ++p)
        if (*p==x)
                ++count;
    return count;
}
```

Note how we can move a pointer to point to the next element of an array using **++** and that we can leave out the initializer in a **for**-statement if we don't need it.

The definition of count_x() assumes that the char* is a *C-style string*, that is, that the pointer points to a zero-terminated array of char.

In older code, 0 or NULL is typically used instead of nullptr. However, using nullptr eliminates potential confusion between integers (such as 0 or NULL) and pointers (such as nullptr).

In the count_x() example, we are not using the initializer part of the for-statement, so we can use the simpler while-statement:

```
int count_x(char* p, char x)
    // count the number of occurrences of x in p[]
    // p is assumed to point to a zero-terminated array of char (or to nothing)
{
    if (p==nullptr) return 0;
    int count = 0;
    while (*p) {
        if (*p==x)
            ++count;
        ++p;
    }
    return count;
}
```

The while-statement executes until its condition becomes false.

A test of a numeric value (e.g., while (*p) in count_x()) is equivalent to comparing the value to 0 (e.g., while (*p!=0)). A test of a pointer value (e.g., if (p)) is equivalent to comparing the value to nullptr (e.g., if (p!=nullptr)).

1.9 Tests

C++ provides a conventional set of statements for expressing selection and looping. For example, here is a simple function that prompts the user and returns a Boolean indicating the response:

```
bool accept()
{
    cout << "Do you want to proceed (y or n)?\n";   // write question

    char answer = 0;                                // initialize to a value that will not appear on input
    cin >> answer;                                  // read answer

    if (answer == 'y')
        return true;
    return false;
}
```

To match the << output operator ("put to"), the >> operator ("get from") is used for input; cin is the standard input stream (Chapter 8). The type of the right-hand operand of >> determines what input is accepted, and its right-hand operand is the target of the input operation. The \n character at the end of the output string represents a newline (§1.3).

Note that the definition of **answer** appears where it is needed (and not before that). A declaration can appear anywhere a statement can.

The example could be improved by taking an **n** (for "no") answer into account:

```
bool accept2()
{
    cout << "Do you want to proceed (y or n)?\n";     // write question

    char answer = 0;                                   // initialize to a value that will not appear on input
    cin >> answer;                                     // read answer

    switch (answer) {
    case 'y':
        return true;
    case 'n':
        return false;
    default:
        cout << "I'll take that for a no.\n";
        return false;
    }
}
```

A **switch**-statement tests a value against a set of constants. The case constants must be distinct, and if the value tested does not match any of them, the **default** is chosen. If no **default** is provided, no action is taken if the value doesn't match any case constant.

We don't have to exit a **case** by returning from the function that contains its **switch**-statement. Often, we just want to continue execution with the statement following the **switch**-statement. We can do that using a **break** statement. As an example, consider an overly clever, yet primitive, parser for a trivial command video game:

```
void action()
{
    while (true) {
        cout << "enter action:\n";       // request action
        string act;
        cin >> act;              // read characters into a string
        Point delta {0,0};       // Point holds an {x,y} pair

        for (char ch : act) {
            switch (ch) {
            case 'u':  // up
            case 'n':  // north
                ++delta.y;
                break;
            case 'r':   // right
            case 'e':   // east
                ++delta.x;
                break;
            // ... more actions ...
```

```
            default:
                cout << "I freeze!\n";
            }
            move(current+delta*scale);
            update_display();
        }
    }
}
```

1.10 Advice

[1]   The material in this chapter roughly corresponds to what is described in much greater detail in Chapters 5-6, 9-10, and 12 of [Stroustrup,2013].

[2]   Don't panic! All will become clear in time; §1.1.

[3]   You don't have to know every detail of C++ to write good programs.

[4]   Focus on programming techniques, not on language features.

[5]   For the final word on language definition issues, see the ISO C++ standard; §14.1.3.

[6]   "Package" meaningful operations as carefully named functions; §1.4.

[7]   A function should perform a single logical operation; §1.4.

[8]   Keep functions short; §1.4.

[9]   Use overloading when functions perform conceptually the same task on different types; §1.4.

[10]   If a function may have to be evaluated at compile time, declare it **constexpr**; §1.7.

[11]   Avoid "magic constants;" use symbolic constants; §1.7.

[12]   Declare one name (only) per declaration.

[13]   Keep common and local names short, and keep uncommon and nonlocal names longer.

[14]   Avoid similar-looking names.

[15]   Avoid **ALL_CAPS** names.

[16]   Prefer the {}-initializer syntax for declarations with a named type; §1.5.

[17]   Prefer the = syntax for the initialization in declarations using **auto**; §1.5.

[18]   Avoid uninitialized variables; §1.5.

[19]   Keep scopes small; §1.6.

[20]   Keep use of pointers simple and straightforward; §1.8.

[21]   Use **nullptr** rather than **0** or **NULL**; §1.8.

[22]   Don't declare a variable until you have a value to initialize it with; §1.8, §1.9.

[23]   Don't say in comments what can be clearly stated in code.

[24]   State intent in comments.

[25]   Maintain a consistent indentation style.

[26]   Avoid complicated expressions.

[27]   Avoid narrowing conversions; §1.5.

2

User-Defined Types

Don't Panic!
– Douglas Adams

- Introduction
- Structures
- Classes
- Unions
- Enumerations
- Advice

2.1 Introduction

We call the types that can be built from the fundamental types (§1.5), the const modifier (§1.7), and the declarator operators (§1.8) *built-in types*. C++'s set of built-in types and operations is rich, but deliberately low-level. They directly and efficiently reflect the capabilities of conventional computer hardware. However, they don't provide the programmer with high-level facilities to conveniently write advanced applications. Instead, C++ augments the built-in types and operations with a sophisticated set of *abstraction mechanisms* out of which programmers can build such high-level facilities. The C++ abstraction mechanisms are primarily designed to let programmers design and implement their own types, with suitable representations and operations, and for programmers to simply and elegantly use such types. Types built out of the built-in types using C++'s abstraction mechanisms are called *user-defined types*. They are referred to as classes and enumerations. Most of this book is devoted to the design, implementation, and use of user-defined types. The rest of this chapter presents the simplest and most fundamental facilities for that. Chapters 4-5 are a more complete description of the abstraction mechanisms and the programming styles they support. Chapters 6-13 present an overview of the standard library, and since the standard library mainly consists of user-defined types, they provide examples of what can be built using the language facilities and programming techniques presented in Chapters 1-5.

2.2 Structures

The first step in building a new type is often to organize the elements it needs into a data structure, a **struct**:

```
struct Vector {
        int sz;         // number of elements
        double* elem;   // pointer to elements
};
```

This first version of **Vector** consists of an **int** and a **double***.

A variable of type **Vector** can be defined like this:

```
Vector v;
```

However, by itself that is not of much use because **v**'s **elem** pointer doesn't point to anything. To be useful, we must give **v** some elements to point to. For example, we can construct a **Vector** like this:

```
void vector_init(Vector& v, int s)
{
        v.elem = new double[s];  // allocate an array of s doubles
        v.sz = s;
}
```

That is, **v**'s **elem** member gets a pointer produced by the **new** operator and **v**'s **sz** member gets the number of elements. The **&** in **Vector&** indicates that we pass **v** by non-**const** reference (§1.8); that way, **vector_init()** can modify the vector passed to it.

The **new** operator allocates memory from an area called *the free store* (also known as *dynamic memory* and *heap*). Objects allocated on the free store are independent of the scope from which they are created and "live" until they are destroyed using the **delete** operator (§4.2.2).

A simple use of **Vector** looks like this:

```
double read_and_sum(int s)
        // read s integers from cin and return their sum; s is assumed to be positive
{
        Vector v;
        vector_init(v,s);           // allocate s elements for v
        for (int i=0; i!=s; ++i)
                cin>>v.elem[i];     // read into elements

        double sum = 0;
        for (int i=0; i!=s; ++i)
                sum+=v.elem[i];     // take the sum of the elements
        return sum;
}
```

There is a long way to go before our **Vector** is as elegant and flexible as the standard-library **vector**. In particular, a user of **Vector** has to know every detail of **Vector**'s representation. The rest of this chapter and the next two gradually improve **Vector** as an example of language features and techniques. Chapter 9 presents the standard-library **vector**, which contains many nice improvements.

I use **vector** and other standard-library components as examples
- to illustrate language features and design techniques, and
- to help you learn and use the standard-library components.

Don't reinvent standard-library components, such as **vector** and **string**; use them.

We use . (dot) to access **struct** members through a name (and through a reference) and –> to access **struct** members through a pointer. For example:

```
void f(Vector v, Vector& rv, Vector* pv)
{
    int i1 = v.sz;        // access through name
    int i2 = rv.sz;       // access through reference
    int i4 = pv->sz;      // access through pointer
}
```

2.3 Classes

Having the data specified separately from the operations on it has advantages, such as the ability to use the data in arbitrary ways. However, a tighter connection between the representation and the operations is needed for a user-defined type to have all the properties expected of a "real type." In particular, we often want to keep the representation inaccessible to users, so as to ease use, guarantee consistent use of the data, and allow us to later improve the representation. To do that we have to distinguish between the interface to a type (to be used by all) and its implementation (which has access to the otherwise inaccessible data). The language mechanism for that is called a *class*. A class is defined to have a set of *members*, which can be data, function, or type members. The interface is defined by the **public** members of a class, and **private** members are accessible only through that interface. For example:

```
class Vector {
public:
    Vector(int s) :elem{new double[s]}, sz{s} { }   // construct a Vector
    double& operator[](int i) { return elem[i]; }    // element access: subscripting
    int size() { return sz; }
private:
    double* elem;  // pointer to the elements
    int sz;        // the number of elements
};
```

Given that, we can define a variable of our new type **Vector**:

```
Vector v(6);     // a Vector with 6 elements
```

We can illustrate a **Vector** object graphically:

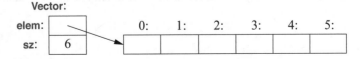

Basically, the Vector object is a "handle" containing a pointer to the elements (elem) and the number of elements (sz). The number of elements (6 in the example) can vary from Vector object to Vector object, and a Vector object can have a different number of elements at different times (§4.2.3). However, the Vector object itself is always the same size. This is the basic technique for handling varying amounts of information in C++: a fixed-size handle referring to a variable amount of data "elsewhere" (e.g., on the free store allocated by new; §4.2.2). How to design and use such objects is the main topic of Chapter 4.

Here, the representation of a Vector (the members elem and sz) is accessible only through the interface provided by the public members: Vector(), operator[](), and size(). The read_and_sum() example from §2.2 simplifies to:

```
double read_and_sum(int s)
{
    Vector v(s);                    // make a vector of s elements
    for (int i=0; i!=v.size(); ++i)
        cin>>v[i];                  // read into elements

    double sum = 0;
    for (int i=0; i!=v.size(); ++i)
        sum+=v[i];                  // take the sum of the elements
    return sum;
}
```

A "function" with the same name as its class is called a *constructor*, that is, a function used to construct objects of a class. So, the constructor, Vector(), replaces vector_init() from §2.2. Unlike an ordinary function, a constructor is guaranteed to be used to initialize objects of its class. Thus, defining a constructor eliminates the problem of uninitialized variables for a class.

Vector(int) defines how objects of type Vector are constructed. In particular, it states that it needs an integer to do that. That integer is used as the number of elements. The constructor initializes the Vector members using a member initializer list:

```
:elem{new double[s]}, sz{s}
```

That is, we first initialize elem with a pointer to s elements of type double obtained from the free store. Then, we initialize sz to s.

Access to elements is provided by a subscript function, called operator[]. It returns a reference to the appropriate element (a double&).

The size() function is supplied to give users the number of elements.

Obviously, error handling is completely missing, but we'll return to that in §3.4. Similarly, we did not provide a mechanism to "give back" the array of doubles acquired by new; §4.2.2 shows how to use a destructor to elegantly do that.

There is no fundamental difference between a struct and a class; a struct is simply a class with members public by default. For example, you can define constructors and other member functions for a struct.

2.4 Unions

A **union** is a **struct** in which all members are allocated at the same address so that the **union** occupies only as much space as its largest member. Naturally, a **union** can hold a value for only one member at a time. For example, consider a symbol table entry that holds a name and a value:

```
enum Type { str, num };

struct Entry {
    char* name;
    Type t;
    char* s;   // use s if t==str
    int i;       // use i if t==num
};

void f(Entry* p)
{
    if (p->t == str)
        cout << p->s;
    // ...
}
```

The members **s** and **i** can never be used at the same time, so space is wasted. It can be easily recovered by specifying that both should be members of a **union**, like this:

```
union Value {
    char* s;
    int i;
};
```

The language doesn't keep track of which kind of value is held by a **union**, so the programmer must do that:

```
struct Entry {
    char* name;
    Type t;
    Value v;   // use v.s if t==str; use v.i if t==num
};

void f(Entry* p)
{
    if (p->t == str)
        cout << p->v.s;
    // ...
}
```

Maintaining the correspondence between a *type field* (here, **t**) and the type held in a **union** is error-prone. To avoid errors, one can encapsulate a **union** so that the correspondence between a type field and access to the **union** members is guaranteed. At the application level, abstractions relying on such *tagged unions* are common and useful, but use of "naked" **union**s is best minimized.

2.5 Enumerations

In addition to classes, C++ supports a simple form of user-defined type for which we can enumer-ate the values:

```
enum class Color { red, blue, green };
enum class Traffic_light { green, yellow, red };

Color col = Color::red;
Traffic_light light = Traffic_light::red;
```

Note that enumerators (e.g., **red**) are in the scope of their **enum class**, so that they can be used repeatedly in different **enum class**es without confusion. For example, **Color::red** is **Color**'s **red** which is different from **Traffic_light::red**.

Enumerations are used to represent small sets of integer values. They are used to make code more readable and less error-prone than it would have been had the symbolic (and mnemonic) enu-merator names not been used.

The **class** after the **enum** specifies that an enumeration is strongly typed and that its enumerators are scoped. Being separate types, **enum class**es help prevent accidental misuses of constants. In particular, we cannot mix **Traffic_light** and **Color** values:

```
Color x = red;                  // error: which red?
Color y = Traffic_light::red;   // error: that red is not a Color
Color z = Color::red;           // OK
```

Similarly, we cannot implicitly mix **Color** and integer values:

```
int i = Color::red;             // error: Color::red is not an int
Color c = 2;                    // error: 2 is not a Color
```

By default, an **enum class** has only assignment, initialization, and comparisons (e.g., **==** and **<**; §1.5) defined. However, an enumeration is a user-defined type so we can define operators for it:

```
Traffic_light& operator++(Traffic_light& t)
    // prefix increment: ++
{
    switch (t) {
    case Traffic_light::green:     return t=Traffic_light::yellow;
    case Traffic_light::yellow:    return t=Traffic_light::red;
    case Traffic_light::red:       return t=Traffic_light::green;
    }
}

Traffic_light next = ++light;       // next becomes Traffic_light::green
```

If you don't want to explicitly qualify enumerator names and want enumerator values to be **ints** (without the need for an explicit conversion), you can remove the **class** from **enum class** to get a "plain" enum. The enumerators from a "plain" **enum** are entered into the same scope as the name of their **enum** and implicitly converts to their integer value. For example:

```
enum Color { red, green, blue };
int col = green;
```

Here col gets the value 1. By default, the integer values of enumerators starts with 0 and increases by one for each additional enumerator. The "plain" enums have been in C++ (and C) from the earliest days, so even though they are less well behaved, they are common in current code.

2.6 Advice

[1]   The material in this chapter roughly corresponds to what is described in much greater detail in Chapter 8 of [Stroustrup,2013].

[2]   Organize related data into structures (structs or classes); §2.2.

[3]   Represent the distinction between an interface and an implemetation using a class; §2.3.

[4]   A struct is simply a class with its members public by default; §2.3.

[5]   Define constructors to guarantee and simplify initialization of classes; §2.3.

[6]   Avoid "naked" unions; wrap them in a class together with a type field; §2.4.

[7]   Use enumerations to represent sets of named constants; §2.5.

[8]   Prefer class enums over "plain" enums to minimize surprises; §2.5.

[9]   Define operations on enumerations for safe and simple use; §2.5.

3

Modularity

Don't interrupt me while I'm interrupting.
– Winston S. Churchill

- Introduction
- Separate Compilation
- Namespaces
- Error Handling
    Exceptions; Invariants; Static Assertions
- Advice

3.1 Introduction

A C++ program consists of many separately developed parts, such as functions (§1.3), user-defined types (Chapter 2), class hierarchies (§4.5), and templates (Chapter 5). The key to managing this is to clearly define the interactions among those parts. The first and most important step is to distinguish between the interface to a part and its implementation. At the language level, C++ represents interfaces by declarations. A *declaration* specifies all that's needed to use a function or a type. For example:

```
double sqrt(double);      // the square root function takes a double and returns a double

class Vector {
public:
    Vector(int s);
    double& operator[](int i);
    int size();
private:
    double* elem; // elem points to an array of sz doubles
    int sz;
};
```

The key point here is that the function bodies, the function *definitions*, are "elsewhere." For this example, we might like for the representation of Vector to be "elsewhere" also, but we will deal with that later (abstract types; §4.3). The definition of sqrt() will look like this:

```
double sqrt(double d)          // definition of sqrt()
{
        // ... algorithm as found in math textbook ...
}
```

For Vector, we need to define all three member functions:

```
Vector::Vector(int s)                  // definition of the constructor
        :elem{new double[s]}, sz{s}    // initialize members
{
}

double& Vector::operator[](int i)      // definition of subscripting
{
        return elem[i];
}

int Vector::size()                     // definition of size()
{
        return sz;
}
```

We must define Vector's functions, but not sqrt() because it is part of the standard library. However, that makes no real difference: a library is simply some "other code we happen to use" written with the same language facilities as we use.

3.2 Separate Compilation

C++ supports a notion of separate compilation where user code sees only declarations of the types and functions used. The definitions of those types and functions are in separate source files and compiled separately. This can be used to organize a program into a set of semi-independent code fragments. Such separation can be used to minimize compilation times and to strictly enforce separation of logically distinct parts of a program (thus minimizing the chance of errors). A library is often a collection of separately compiled code fragments (e.g., functions).

Typically, we place the declarations that specify the interface to a module in a file with a name indicating its intended use. For example:

```
// Vector.h:

class Vector {
public:
        Vector(int s);
        double& operator[](int i);
        int size();
```

```
    private:
        double* elem;          // elem points to an array of sz doubles
        int sz;
};
```

This declaration would be placed in a file Vector.h, and users will *include* that file, called a *header file*, to access that interface. For example:

```
// user.cpp:

#include "Vector.h"        // get Vector's interface
#include <cmath>           // get the the standard-library math function interface including sqrt()

using namespace std;       // make std members visible (§3.3)

double sqrt_sum(Vector& v)
{
    double sum = 0;
    for (int i=0; i!=v.size(); ++i)
        sum+=sqrt(v[i]);              // sum of square roots
    return sum;
}
```

To help the compiler ensure consistency, the .cpp file providing the implementation of Vector will also include the .h file providing its interface:

```
// Vector.cpp:

#include "Vector.h" // get the interface

Vector::Vector(int s)
    :elem{new double[s]}, sz{s}      // initialize members
{
}

double& Vector::operator[](int i)
{
    return elem[i];
}

int Vector::size()
{
    return sz;
}
```

The code in user.cpp and Vector.cpp shares the Vector interface information presented in Vector.h, but the two files are otherwise independent and can be separately compiled. Graphically, the program fragments can be represented like this:

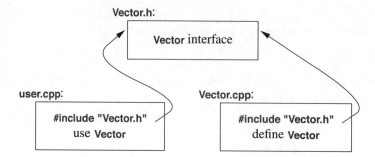

Strictly speaking, using separate compilation isn't a language issue; it is an issue of how best to take advantage of a particular language implementation. However, it is of great practical importance. The best approach is to maximize modularity, represent that modularity logically through language features, and then exploit the modularity physically through files for effective separate compilation.

3.3 Namespaces

In addition to functions (§1.4), classes (§2.3), and enumerations (§2.5), C++ offers *namespaces* as a mechanism for expressing that some declarations belong together and that their names shouldn't clash with other names. For example, I might want to experiment with my own complex number type (§4.2.1, §12.4):

```
namespace My_code {
    class complex {
        // ...
    };

    complex sqrt(complex);
    // ...

    int main();
}

int My_code::main()
{
    complex z {1,2};
    auto z2 = sqrt(z);
    std::cout << '{' << z2.real() << ',' << z2.imag() << "}\n";
    // ...
}

int main()
{
    return My_code::main();
}
```

By putting my code into the namespace My_code, I make sure that my names do not conflict with the standard-library names in namespace std (§3.3). The precaution is wise, because the standard library does provide support for complex arithmetic (§4.2.1, §12.4).

The simplest way to access a name in another namespace is to qualify it with the namespace name (e.g., std::cout and My_code::main). The "real main()" is defined in the global namespace, that is, not local to a defined namespace, class, or function. To gain access to names in the standard-library namespace, we can use a using-directive:

```
using namespace std;
```

A using-directive makes names from the named namespace accessible as if they were local to the scope in which we placed the directive. So after the using-directive for std, we can simply write cout rather than std::cout.

Namespaces are primarily used to organize larger program components, such as libraries. They simplify the composition of a program out of separately developed parts.

3.4 Error Handling

Error handling is a large and complex topic with concerns and ramifications that go far beyond language facilities into programming techniques and tools. However, C++ provides a few features to help. The major tool is the type system itself. Instead of painstakingly building up our applications from the built-in types (e.g., char, int, and double) and statements (e.g., if, while, and for), we build more types that are appropriate for our applications (e.g., string, map, and regex) and algorithms (e.g., sort(), find_if(), and draw_all()). Such higher-level constructs simplify our programming, limit our opportunities for mistakes (e.g., you are unlikely to try to apply a tree traversal to a dialog box), and increase the compiler's chances of catching such errors. The majority of C++ constructs are dedicated to the design and implementation of elegant and efficient abstractions (e.g., user-defined types and algorithms using them). One effect of this modularity and abstraction (in particular, the use of libraries) is that the point where a run-time error can be detected is separated from the point where it can be handled. As programs grow, and especially when libraries are used extensively, standards for handling errors become important. It is a good idea to design and articulate a strategy for error handling early on in the development of a program.

3.4.1 Exceptions

Consider again the Vector example. What *ought* to be done when we try to access an element that is out of range for the vector from §2.3?

- The writer of Vector doesn't know what the user would like to have done in this case (the writer of Vector typically doesn't even know in which program the vector will be running).
- The user of Vector cannot consistently detect the problem (if the user could, the out-of-range access wouldn't happen in the first place).

The solution is for the Vector implementer to detect the attempted out-of-range access and then tell the user about it. The user can then take appropriate action. For example, Vector::operator[]() can detect an attempted out-of-range access and throw an out_of_range exception:

```
double& Vector::operator[](int i)
{
    if (i<0 || size()<=i)
        throw out_of_range{"Vector::operator[]"};
    return elem[i];
}
```

The **throw** transfers control to a handler for exceptions of type **out_of_range** in some function that directly or indirectly called **Vector::operator[]()**. To do that, the implementation will *unwind* the function call stack as needed to get back to the context of that caller. That is, the exception handling mechanism will exit scopes and function as needed to get back to a caller that has expressed interest in handling that kind of exception, invoking destructors (§4.2.2) along the way as needed. For example:

```
void f(Vector& v)
{
    // ...
    try { // exceptions here are handled by the handler defined below

        v[v.size()] = 7;  // try to access beyond the end of v
    }
    catch (out_of_range) {    // oops: out_of_range error
        // ... handle range error ...
    }
    // ...
}
```

We put code for which we are interested in handling exceptions into a **try**-block. That attempted assignment to v[v.size()] will fail. Therefore, the **catch**-clause providing a handler for **out_of_range** will be entered. The **out_of_range** type is defined in the standard library (in **<stdexcept>**) and is in fact used by some standard-library container access functions.

Use of the exception-handling mechanisms can make error handling simpler, more systematic, and more readable. To achieve that don't overuse **try**-statements. The main technique for making error handling simple and systematic (called *Resource Aquisition Is Initialization*) is explained in §4.2.2.

A function that should never throw an exception can be declared **noexcept**. For example:

```
void user(int sz) noexcept
{
    Vector v(sz);
    iota(&v[0],&v[sz],1); // fill v with 1,2,3,4...
    // ...
}
```

If all good intent and planning fails, so that **user()** still throws, the standard-library function **terminate()** is called to immediately terminate the program.

3.4.2 Invariants

The use of exceptions to signal out-of-range access is an example of a function checking its argument and refusing to act because a basic assumption, a *precondition*, didn't hold. Had we formally specified **Vector**'s subscript operator, we would have said something like "the index must be in the [0:size()) range," and that was in fact what we tested in our **operator[]()**. The [a:b) notation specifies a half-open range, meaning that **a** is part of the range, but **b** is not. Whenever we define a function, we should consider what its preconditions are and if feasible test them.

However, **operator[]()** operates on objects of type **Vector** and nothing it does makes any sense unless the members of **Vector** have "reasonable" values. In particular, we did say "**elem** points to an array of **sz** doubles" but we only said that in a comment. Such a statement of what is assumed to be true for a class is called a *class invariant*, or simply an *invariant*. It is the job of a constructor to establish the invariant for its class (so that the member functions can rely on it) and for the member functions to make sure that the invariant holds when they exit. Unfortunately, our **Vector** constructor only partially did its job. It properly initialized the **Vector** members, but it failed to check that the arguments passed to it made sense. Consider:

```
Vector v(–27);
```

This is likely to cause chaos.

Here is a more appropriate definition:

```
Vector::Vector(int s)
{
    if (s<0)
        throw length_error{"Vector constructor: negative size"};
    elem = new double[s];
    sz = s;
}
```

I use the standard-library exception **length_error** to report a non-positive number of elements because some standard-library operations use that exception to report problems of this kind. If operator **new** can't find memory to allocate, it throws a **std::bad_alloc**. We can now write:

```
void test()
{
    try {
        Vector v(–27);
    }
    catch (std::length_error) {
        // handle negative size
    }
    catch (std::bad_alloc) {
        // handle memory exhaustion
    }
}
```

You can define your own classes to be used as exceptions and have them carry arbitrary information from a point where an error is detected to a point where it can be handled (§3.4.1).

Often, a function has no way of completing its assigned task after an exception is thrown. Then, "handling" an exception simply means doing some minimal local cleanup and rethrowing the exception. To throw (*rethrow*) the exception caught in an exception handler, we simply write throw;. For example:

```
void test()
{
    try {
        Vector v(–27);
    }
    catch (std::length_error) {
        cout << "test failed: length error\n";
        throw;      // rethrow
    }
    catch (std::bad_alloc) {
        // Ouch! test() is not designed to handle memory exhaustion
        std::terminate();      // terminate the program
    }
}
```

The notion of invariants is central to the design of classes, and preconditions serve a similar role in the design of functions. Invariants

- help us to understand precisely what we want
- force us to be specific; that gives us a better chance of getting our code correct (after debugging and testing).

The notion of invariants underlies C++'s notions of resource management supported by constructors (Chapter 4) and destructors (§4.2.2, §11.2).

3.4.3 Static Assertions

Exceptions report errors found at run time. If an error can be found at compile time, it is usually preferable to do so. That's what much of the type system and the facilities for specifying the interfaces to user-defined types are for. However, we can also perform simple checks on other properties that are known at compile time and report failures as compiler error messages. For example:

```
static_assert(4<=sizeof(int), "integers are too small");   // check integer size
```

This will write integers are too small if 4<=sizeof(int) does not hold, that is, if an int on this system does not have at least 4 bytes. We call such statements of expectations *assertions*.

The static_assert mechanism can be used for anything that can be expressed in terms of constant expressions (§1.7). For example:

```
constexpr double C = 299792.458;              // km/s

void f(double speed)
{
    const double local_max = 160.0/(60*60);        // 160 km/h == 160.0/(60*60) km/s
```

```
        static_assert(speed<C,"can't go that fast");     // error: speed must be a constant
        static_assert(local_max<C,"can't go that fast"); // OK

    // ...
}
```

In general, static_assert(A,S) prints S as a compiler error message if A is not true.

The most important uses of static_assert come when we make assertions about types used as parameters in generic programming (§5.4, §11.6).

For runtime-checked assertions, use exceptions.

3.5 Advice

[1]   The material in this chapter roughly corresponds to what is described in much greater detail in Chapters 13-15 of [Stroustrup,2013].

[2]   Distinguish between declarations (used as interfaces) and definitions (used as implementations); §3.1.

[3]   Use header files to represent interfaces and to emphasize logical structure; §3.2.

[4]   #include a header in the source file that implements its functions; §3.2.

[5]   Avoid non-inline function definitions in headers; §3.2.

[6]   Use namespaces to express logical structure; §3.3.

[7]   Use using-directives for transition, for foundational libraries (such as std), or within a local scope; §3.3.

[8]   Don't put a using-directive in a header file; §3.3.

[9]   Throw an exception to indicate that you cannot perform an assigned task; §3.4.

[10] Use exceptions for error handling; §3.4.

[11] Develop an error-handling strategy early in a design; §3.4.

[12] Use purpose-designed user-defined types as exceptions (not built-in types); §3.4.1.

[13] Don't try to catch every exception in every function; §3.4.

[14] If your function may not throw, declare it noexcept; §3.4.

[15] Let a constructor establish an invariant, and throw if it cannot; §3.4.2.

[16] Design your error-handling strategy around invariants; §3.4.2.

[17] What can be checked at compile time is usually best checked at compile time (using static_assert); §3.4.3.

4

Classes

*Those types are not "abstract";
they are as real as* int *and* float.
— *Doug McIlroy*

- Introduction
- Concrete Types
    An Arithmetic Type; A Container; Initializing Containers
- Abstract Types
- Virtual Functions
- Class Hierarchies
    Explicit Overriding; Benefits from Hierarchies; Hierarchy Navigation; Avoiding
    Resource Leaks
- Copy and Move
    Copying Containers; Moving Containers; Essential Operations; Resource Management;
    Suppressing Operations
- Advice

4.1 Introduction

This chapter and the next aim to give you an idea of C++'s support for abstraction and resource management without going into a lot of detail:

- This chapter informally presents ways of defining and using new types (*user-defined types*). In particular, it presents the basic properties, implementation techniques, and language facilities used for *concrete classes*, *abstract classes*, and *class hierarchies*.
- The next chapter introduces templates as a mechanism for parameterizing types and algorithms with (other) types and algorithms. Computations on user-defined and built-in types are represented as functions, sometimes generalized to *template functions* and *function objects*.

These are the language facilities supporting the programming styles known as *object-oriented programming* and *generic programming*. Chapters 6-13 follow up by presenting examples of standard-library facilities and their use.

The central language feature of C++ is the *class*. A class is a user-defined type provided to represent a concept in the code of a program. Whenever our design for a program has a useful concept, idea, entity, etc., we try to represent it as a class in the program so that the idea is there in the code, rather than just in our head, in a design document, or in some comments. A program built out of a well chosen set of classes is far easier to understand and get right than one that builds everything directly in terms of the built-in types. In particular, classes are often what libraries offer.

Essentially all language facilities beyond the fundamental types, operators, and statements exist to help define better classes or to use them more conveniently. By "better," I mean more correct, easier to maintain, more efficient, more elegant, easier to use, easier to read, and easier to reason about. Most programming techniques rely on the design and implementation of specific kinds of classes. The needs and tastes of programmers vary immensely. Consequently, the support for classes is extensive. Here, we will just consider the basic support for three important kinds of classes:

- Concrete classes (§4.2)
- Abstract classes (§4.3)
- Classes in class hierarchies (§4.5)

An astounding number of useful classes turn out to be of these three kinds. Even more classes can be seen as simple variants of these kinds or are implemented using combinations of the techniques used for these.

4.2 Concrete Types

The basic idea of *concrete classes* is that they behave "just like built-in types." For example, a complex number type and an infinite-precision integer are much like built-in int, except of course that they have their own semantics and sets of operations. Similarly, a vector and a string are much like built-in arrays, except that they are better behaved (§7.2, §8.3, §9.2).

The defining characteristic of a concrete type is that its representation is part of its definition. In many important cases, such as a vector, that representation is only one or more pointers to data stored elsewhere, but it is present in each object of a concrete class. That allows implementations to be optimally efficient in time and space. In particular, it allows us to

- place objects of concrete types on the stack, in statically allocated memory, and in other objects (§1.6);
- refer to objects directly (and not just through pointers or references);
- initialize objects immediately and completely (e.g., using constructors; §2.3); and
- copy objects (§4.6).

The representation can be private (as it is for Vector; §2.3) and accessible only through the member functions, but it is present. Therefore, if the representation changes in any significant way, a user must recompile. This is the price to pay for having concrete types behave exactly like built-in types. For types that don't change often, and where local variables provide much-needed clarity and efficiency, this is acceptable and often ideal. To increase flexibility, a concrete type can keep major parts of its representation on the free store (dynamic memory, heap) and access them through the part stored in the class object itself. That's the way **vector** and **string** are implemented; they can be considered resource handles with carefully crafted interfaces.

4.2.1 An Arithmetic Type

The "classical user-defined arithmetic type" is **complex**:

```
class complex {
      double re, im;  // representation: two doubles
public:
      complex(double r, double i) :re{r}, im{i} {}    // construct complex from two scalars
      complex(double r) :re{r}, im{0} {}              // construct complex from one scalar
      complex() :re{0}, im{0} {}                      // default complex: {0,0}

      double real() const { return re; }
      void real(double d) { re=d; }
      double imag() const { return im; }
      void imag(double d) { im=d; }

      complex& operator+=(complex z) { re+=z.re, im+=z.im; return *this; }   // add to re and im
                                                                            // and return the result
      complex& operator-=(complex z) { re-=z.re, im-=z.im; return *this; }

      complex& operator*=(complex);    // defined out-of-class somewhere
      complex& operator/=(complex);    // defined out-of-class somewhere
};
```

This is a slightly simplified version of the standard-library **complex** (§12.4). The class definition itself contains only the operations requiring access to the representation. The representation is simple and conventional. For practical reasons, it has to be compatible with what Fortran provided 50 years ago, and we need a conventional set of operators. In addition to the logical demands, **complex** must be efficient or it will remain unused. This implies that simple operations must be inlined. That is, simple operations (such as constructors, +=, and imag()) must be implemented without function calls in the generated machine code. Functions defined in a class are inlined by default. It is possible to explicitly request inlining by preceeding a function declaration with the keyword **inline**. An industrial-strength **complex** (like the standard-library one) is carefully implemented to do appropriate inlining.

A constructor that can be invoked without an argument is called a *default constructor*. Thus, **complex()** is **complex**'s default constructor. By defining a default constructor you eliminate the possibility of uninitialized variables of that type.

The **const** specifiers on the functions returning the real and imaginary parts indicate that these functions do not modify the object for which they are called.

Many useful operations do not require direct access to the representation of **complex**, so they can be defined separately from the class definition:

```
complex operator+(complex a, complex b) { return a+=b; }
complex operator–(complex a, complex b) { return a–=b; }
complex operator–(complex a) { return {–a.real(), –a.imag()}; }      // unary minus
complex operator*(complex a, complex b) { return a*=b; }
complex operator/(complex a, complex b) { return a/=b; }
```

Here, I use the fact that an argument passed by value is copied, so that I can modify an argument without affecting the caller's copy, and use the result as the return value.

The definitions of == and != are straightforward:

```
bool operator==(complex a, complex b)          // equal
{
      return a.real()==b.real() && a.imag()==b.imag();
}


bool operator!=(complex a, complex b)          // not equal
{
      return !(a==b);
}


complex sqrt(complex);        // the definition is elsewhere

// ...
```

Class complex can be used like this:

```
void f(complex z)
{
      complex a {2.3};          // construct {2.3,0.0} from 2.3
      complex b {1/a};
      complex c {a+z*complex{1,2.3}};
      // ...
      if (c != b)
            c = –(b/a)+2*b;
}
```

The compiler converts operators involving complex numbers into appropriate function calls. For example, c!=b means operator!=(c,b) and 1/a means operator/(complex{1},a).

User-defined operators ("overloaded operators") should be used cautiously and conventionally. The syntax is fixed by the language, so you can't define a unary /. Also, it is not possible to change the meaning of an operator for built-in types, so you can't redefine + to subtract ints.

4.2.2 A Container

A *container* is an object holding a collection of elements, so we call Vector a container because it is the type of objects that are containers. As defined in §2.3, Vector isn't an unreasonable container of doubles: it is simple to understand, establishes a useful invariant (§3.4.2), provides range-checked access (§3.4.1), and provides size() to allow us to iterate over its elements. However, it does have a fatal flaw: it allocates elements using new but never deallocates them. That's not a good idea because although C++ defines an interface for a garbage collector (§4.6.4), it is not guaranteed that one is available to make unused memory available for new objects. In some environments you can't use a collector, and sometimes you prefer more precise control of destruction for logical or performance reasons. We need a mechanism to ensure that the memory allocated by the constructor is deallocated; that mechanism is a *destructor*:

```
class Vector {
private:
        double∗ elem;          // elem points to an array of sz doubles
        int sz;
public:
        Vector(int s) :elem{new double[s]}, sz{s}        // constructor: acquire resources
        {
                for (int i=0; i!=s; ++i)          // initialize elements
                        elem[i]=0;
        }

        ˜Vector() { delete[] elem; }                     // destructor: release resources

        double& operator[](int i);
        int size() const;
};
```

The name of a destructor is the complement operator, ˜, followed by the name of the class; it is the complement of a constructor. **Vector**'s constructor allocates some memory on the free store (also called the *heap* or *dynamic store*) using the **new** operator. The destructor cleans up by freeing that memory using the **delete** operator. This is all done without intervention by users of **Vector**. The users simply create and use **Vector**s much as they would variables of built-in types. For example:

```
void fct(int n)
{
        Vector v(n);

        // ... use v ...

        {
                Vector v2(2∗n);
                // ... use v and v2 ...
        } // v2 is destroyed here

        // ... use v ..

} // v is destroyed here
```

Vector obeys the same rules for naming, scope, allocation, lifetime, etc. (§1.6), as does a built-in type, such as **int** and **char**. This **Vector** has been simplified by leaving out error handling; see §3.4.

The constructor/destructor combination is the basis of many elegant techniques. In particular, it is the basis for most C++ general resource management techniques (§11.2). Consider a graphical illustration of a **Vector**:

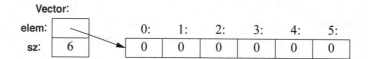

The constructor allocates the elements and initializes the **Vector** members appropriately. The destructor deallocates the elements. This *handle-to-data model* is very commonly used to manage data that can vary in size during the lifetime of an object. The technique of acquiring resources in a constructor and releasing them in a destructor, known as *Resource Acquisition Is Initialization* or *RAII*, allows us to eliminate "naked **new** operations," that is, to avoid allocations in general code and keep them buried inside the implementation of well-behaved abstractions. Similarly, "naked **delete** operations" should be avoided. Avoiding naked **new** and naked **delete** makes code far less error-prone and far easier to keep free of resource leaks (§11.2).

4.2.3 Initializing Containers

A container exists to hold elements, so obviously we need convenient ways of getting elements into a container. We can handle that by creating a **Vector** with an appropriate number of elements and then assigning to them, but typically other ways are more elegant. Here, I just mention two favorites:

- *Initializer-list constructor*: Initialize with a list of elements.
- **push_back()**: Add a new element at the end (at the back of) the sequence.

These can be declared like this:

```
class Vector {
public:
    Vector(std::initializer_list<double>);    // initialize with a list of doubles
    // ...
    void push_back(double);                    // add element at end, increasing the size by one
    // ...
};
```

The **push_back()** is useful for input of arbitrary numbers of elements. For example:

```
Vector read(istream& is)
{
    Vector v;
    for (double d; is>>d;)       // read floating-point values into d
        v.push_back(d);          // add d to v
    return v;
}
```

The input loop is terminated by an end-of-file or a formatting error. Until that happens, each number read is added to the **Vector** so that at the end, **v**'s size is the number of elements read. I used a **for**-statement rather than the more conventional **while**-statement to keep the scope of **d** limited to the loop. The way to provide **Vector** with a move constructor, so that returning a potentially huge amount of data from **read()** is cheap, is explained in §4.6.2.

The std::initializer_list used to define the initializer-list constructor is a standard-library type known to the compiler: when we use a {}-list, such as {1,2,3,4}, the compiler will create an object of type initializer_list to give to the program. So, we can write:

```
Vector v1 = {1,2,3,4,5};        // v1 has 5 elements
Vector v2 = {1.23, 3.45, 6.7, 8};  // v2 has 4 elements
```

Vector's initializer-list constructor might be defined like this:

```
Vector::Vector(std::initializer_list<double> lst)    // initialize with a list
    :elem{new double[lst.size()]}, sz{static_cast<int>(lst.size())}
{
        copy(lst.begin(),lst.end(),elem);    // copy from lst into elem (§10.6)
}
```

I use the ugly static_cast (§14.2.4) to convert the size of the initializer list to an int. This is pedantic because the chance that the number of elements in a hand-written list is larger than the largest integer (32,767 for 16-bit integers and 2,147,483,647 for 32-bit integers) is rather low. However, it is worth remembering that the type system has no common sense. It knows about the possible values of variables, rather than actual values, so it might complain where there is no actual violation. However, sooner or later, such warnings will save the programmer from a bad error.

A static_cast does not check the value it is converting; the programmer is trusted to use it correctly. This is not always a good assumption, so if in doubt, check the value. Explicit type conversions (often called *casts* to remind you that they are used to prop up something broken) are best avoided. Judicious use of the type system and well-designed libraries allow us to eliminate unchecked casts in higher-level software.

4.3 Abstract Types

Types such as complex and Vector are called *concrete types* because their representation is part of their definition. In that, they resemble built-in types. In contrast, an *abstract type* is a type that completely insulates a user from implementation details. To do that, we decouple the interface from the representation and give up genuine local variables. Since we don't know anything about the representation of an abstract type (not even its size), we must allocate objects on the free store (§4.2.2) and access them through references or pointers (§1.8, §11.2.1).

First, we define the interface of a class Container which we will design as a more abstract version of our Vector:

```
class Container {
public:
        virtual double& operator[](int) = 0;    // pure virtual function
        virtual int size() const = 0;    // const member function (§4.2.1)
        virtual ~Container() {}    // destructor (§4.2.2)
};
```

This class is a pure interface to specific containers defined later. The word virtual means "may be redefined later in a class derived from this one." Unsurprisingly, a function declared virtual is called a *virtual function*. A class derived from Container provides an implementation for the

Container interface. The curious =0 syntax says the function is *pure virtual*; that is, some class derived from Container *must* define the function. Thus, it is not possible to define an object that is just a Container; a Container can only serve as the interface to a class that implements its operator[]() and size() functions. A class with a pure virtual function is called an *abstract class*.

This Container can be used like this:

```
void use(Container& c)
{
     const int sz = c.size();

     for (int i=0; i!=sz; ++i)
          cout << c[i] << '\n';
}
```

Note how use() uses the Container interface in complete ignorance of implementation details. It uses size() and [ ] without any idea of exactly which type provides their implementation. A class that provides the interface to a variety of other classes is often called a *polymorphic type*.

As is common for abstract classes, Container does not have a constructor. After all, it does not have any data to initialize. On the other hand, Container does have a destructor and that destructor is virtual. Again, that is common for abstract classes because they tend to be manipulated through references or pointers, and someone destroying a Container through a pointer has no idea what resources are owned by its implementation; see also §4.5.

A container that implements the functions required by the interface defined by the abstract class Container could use the concrete class Vector:

```
class Vector_container : public Container {    // Vector_container implements Container
     Vector v;
public:
     Vector_container(int s) : v(s) { }       // Vector of s elements
     ~Vector_container() {}

     double& operator[](int i) { return v[i]; }
     int size() const { return v.size(); }
};
```

The :public can be read as "is derived from" or "is a subtype of." Class Vector_container is said to be *derived* from class Container, and class Container is said to be a *base* of class Vector_container. An alternative terminology calls Vector_container and Container *subclass* and *superclass*, respectively. The derived class is said to inherit members from its base class, so the use of base and derived classes is commonly referred to as *inheritance*.

The members operator[]() and size() are said to *override* the corresponding members in the base class Container. The destructor (~Vector_container()) overrides the base class destructor (~Container()). Note that the member destructor (~Vector()) is implicitly invoked by its class's destructor (~Vector_container()).

For a function like use(Container&) to use a Container in complete ignorance of implementation details, some other function will have to make an object on which it can operate. For example:

```
void g()
{
    Vector_container vc(10); // ten elements
    // ... fill vc ...
    use(vc);
}
```

Since use() doesn't know about Vector_containers but only knows the Container interface, it will work just as well for a different implementation of a Container. For example:

```
class List_container : public Container {      // List_container implements Container
    std::list<double> ld;      // (standard-library) list of doubles (§9.3)
public:
    List_container() { }       // empty List
    List_container(initializer_list<double> il) : ld{il} { }
    ~List_container() {}

    double& operator[](int i);
    int size() const { return ld.size(); }

};

double& List_container::operator[](int i)
{
    for (auto& x : ld) {
        if (i==0) return x;
        --i;
    }
    throw out_of_range{"List container"};
}
```

Here, the representation is a standard-library list<double>. Usually, I would not implement a container with a subscript operation using a list, because performance of list subscripting is atrocious compared to vector subscripting. However, here I just wanted to show an implementation that is radically different from the usual one.

A function can create a List_container and have use() use it:

```
void h()
{
    List_container lc = { 1, 2, 3, 4, 5, 6, 7, 8, 9 };
    use(lc);
}
```

The point is that use(Container&) has no idea if its argument is a Vector_container, a List_container, or some other kind of container; it doesn't need to know. It can use any kind of Container. It knows only the interface defined by Container. Consequently, use(Container&) needn't be recompiled if the implementation of List_container changes or a brand-new class derived from Container is used.

The flip side of this flexibility is that objects must be manipulated through pointers or references (§4.6, §11.2.1).

4.4   Virtual Functions

Consider again the use of Container:

```
void use(Container& c)
{
    const int sz = c.size();

    for (int i=0; i!=sz; ++i)
        cout << c[i] << '\n';
}
```

How is the call c[i] in use() resolved to the right operator[]()? When h() calls use(), List_container's operator[]() must be called. When g() calls use(), Vector_container's operator[]() must be called. To achieve this resolution, a Container object must contain information to allow it to select the right function to call at run time. The usual implementation technique is for the compiler to convert the name of a virtual function into an index into a table of pointers to functions. That table is usually called the *virtual function table* or simply the vtbl. Each class with virtual functions has its own vtbl identifying its virtual functions. This can be represented graphically like this:

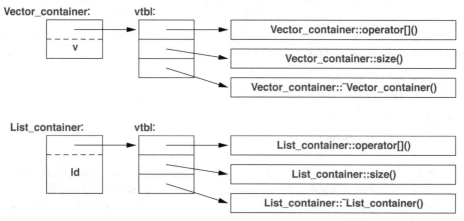

The functions in the vtbl allow the object to be used correctly even when the size of the object and the layout of its data are unknown to the caller. The implementation of the caller needs only to know the location of the pointer to the vtbl in a Container and the index used for each virtual function. This virtual call mechanism can be made almost as efficient as the "normal function call" mechanism (within 25%). Its space overhead is one pointer in each object of a class with virtual functions plus one vtbl for each such class.

4.5   Class Hierarchies

The Container example is a very simple example of a class hierarchy. A *class hierarchy* is a set of classes ordered in a lattice created by derivation (e.g., : public). We use class hierarchies to represent concepts that have hierarchical relationships, such as "A fire engine is a kind of a truck which is a kind of a vehicle" and "A smiley face is a kind of a circle which is a kind of a shape." Huge hierarchies, with hundreds of classes, that are both deep and wide are common. As a semi-realistic classic example, let's consider shapes on a screen:

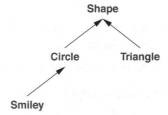

The arrows represent inheritance relationships. For example, class **Circle** is derived from class **Shape**. To represent that simple diagram in code, we must first specify a class that defines the general properties of all shapes:

```
class Shape {
public:
      virtual Point center() const =0;      // pure virtual
      virtual void move(Point to) =0;

      virtual void draw() const = 0;        // draw on current "Canvas"
      virtual void rotate(int angle) = 0;

      virtual ˜Shape() {}                    // destructor
      // ...
};
```

Naturally, this interface is an abstract class: as far as representation is concerned, *nothing* (except the location of the pointer to the **vtbl**) is common for every **Shape**. Given this definition, we can write general functions manipulating vectors of pointers to shapes:

```
void rotate_all(vector<Shape*>& v, int angle) // rotate v's elements by angle degrees
{
     for (auto p : v)
          p–>rotate(angle);
}
```

To define a particular shape, we must say that it is a **Shape** and specify its particular properties (including its virtual functions):

```
class Circle : public Shape {
public:
     Circle(Point p, int rr);            // constructor

     Point center() const { return x; }
     void move(Point to) { x=to; }
```

```
            void draw() const;
            void rotate(int) {}              // nice simple algorithm
    private:
            Point x;    // center
            int r;      // radius
};
```

So far, the `Shape` and `Circle` example provides nothing new compared to the `Container` and `Vector_container` example, but we can build further:

```
class Smiley : public Circle {    // use the circle as the base for a face
public:
        Smiley(Point p, int r) : Circle{p,r}, mouth{nullptr} { }

        ˜Smiley()
        {
            delete mouth;
            for (auto p : eyes)
                delete p;
        }

        void move(Point to);

        void draw() const;
        void rotate(int);

        void add_eye(Shape* s) { eyes.push_back(s); }
        void set_mouth(Shape* s);
        virtual void wink(int i);        // wink eye number i

        // ...

private:
        vector<Shape*> eyes;        // usually two eyes
        Shape* mouth;
};
```

The `push_back()` member function adds its argument to the `vector` (here, `eyes`), increasing that vector's size by one.

We can now define `Smiley::draw()` using calls to `Smiley`'s base and member `draw()`s:

```
void Smiley::draw() const
{
        Circle::draw();
        for (auto p : eyes)
            p–>draw();
        mouth–>draw();
}
```

Note the way that `Smiley` keeps its eyes in a standard-library `vector` and deletes them in its destructor. `Shape`'s destructor is `virtual` and `Smiley`'s destructor overrides it. A virtual destructor is essential for an abstract class because an object of a derived class is usually manipulated through the interface provided by its abstract base class. In particular, it may be deleted through a pointer to a base class. Then, the virtual function call mechanism ensures that the proper destructor is called. That destructor then implicitly invokes the destructors of its bases and members.

In this simplified example, it is the programmer's task to place the eyes and mouth appropriately within the circle representing the face.

We can add data members, operations, or both as we define a new class by derivation. This gives great flexibility with corresponding opportunities for confusion and poor design.

4.5.1 Explicit Overriding

A function in a derived class overrides a virtual function in a base class if that function has exactly the same name and type. In large hierarchies, it is not always obvious if overriding was intended. A function with a slightly different name or a slightly different type may be intended to override or it may be intended to be a separate function. To avoid confusion in such cases, a programmer can explicitly state that a function is meant to override. For example, I could (equivalently) have defined Smiley like this:

```
class Smiley : public Circle {    // use the circle as the base for a face
public:
    Smiley(Point p, int r) : Circle{p,r}, mouth{nullptr} { }

    ~Smiley()
    {
        delete mouth;
        for (auto p : eyes)
            delete p;
    }

    void move(Point to) override;

    void draw() const override;
    void rotate(int) override;

    void add_eye(Shape* s) { eyes.push_back(s); }
    void set_mouth(Shape* s);
    virtual void wink(int i);        // wink eye number i

    // ...

private:
    vector<Shape*> eyes;        // usually two eyes
    Shape* mouth;
};
```

Now, had I mistyped move as mve, I would have gotten an error because no base of Smiley has a virtual function called mve. Similarly, had I added override to the declaration of wink(), I would have gotten an error message.

4.5.2 Benefits from Hierarchies

A class hierarchy offers two kinds of benefits:

- *Interface inheritance*: An object of a derived class can be used wherever an object of a base class is required. That is, the base class acts as an interface for the derived class. The Container and Shape classes are examples. Such classes are often abstract classes.
- *Implementation inheritance*: A base class provides functions or data that simplifies the implementation of derived classes. Smiley's uses of Circle's constructor and of Circle::draw() are examples. Such base classes often have data members and constructors.

Concrete classes – especially classes with small representations – are much like built-in types: we define them as local variables, access them using their names, copy them around, etc. Classes in class hierarchies are different: we tend to allocate them on the free store using new, and we access them through pointers or references. For example, consider a function that reads data describing shapes from an input stream and constructs the appropriate Shape objects:

```
enum class Kind { circle, triangle, smiley };

Shape* read_shape(istream& is)     // read shape descriptions from input stream is
{
    // ... read shape header from is and find its Kind k ...

    switch (k) {
    case Kind::circle:
        // read circle data {Point,int} into p and r
        return new Circle{p,r};
    case Kind::triangle:
        // read triangle data {Point,Point,Point} into p1, p2, and p3
        return new Triangle{p1,p2,p3};
    case Kind::smiley:
        // read smiley data {Point,int,Shape,Shape,Shape} into p, r, e1, e2, and m
        Smiley* ps = new Smiley{p,r};
        ps->add_eye(e1);
        ps->add_eye(e2);
        ps->set_mouth(m);
        return ps;
    }
}
```

A program may use that shape reader like this:

```
void user()
{
    std::vector<Shape*> v;
    while (cin)
        v.push_back(read_shape(cin));
    draw_all(v);                // call draw() for each element
    rotate_all(v,45);           // call rotate(45) for each element
    for (auto p : v)            // remember to delete elements
        delete p;
}
```

Obviously, the example is simplified – especially with respect to error handling – but it vividly illustrates that **user()** has absolutely no idea of which kinds of shapes it manipulates. The **user()** code can be compiled once and later used for new **Shapes** added to the program. Note that there are no pointers to the shapes outside **user()**, so **user()** is responsible for deallocating them. This is done with the **delete** operator and relies critically on **Shape**'s virtual destructor. Because that destructor is virtual, **delete** invokes the destructor for the most derived class. This is crucial because a derived class may have acquired all kinds of resources (such as file handles, locks, and output streams) that need to be released. In this case, a **Smiley** deletes its **eyes** and **mouth** objects.

4.5.3 Hierarchy Navigation

The **read_shape()** function returns **Shape∗** so that we can treat all **Shapes** alike. However, what can we do if we want to use a member function that is only provided by a particular derived class, such as **Smiley**'s **wink()**? We can ask "is this **Shape** a kind of **Smiley**?" using the **dynamic_cast** operator:

```
Shape∗ ps {read_shape(cin)};

if (Smiley∗ p = dynamic_cast<Smiley∗>(ps)) { // ... does ps point to a Smiley? ...
    // ... a Smiley; use it
}
else {
    // ... not a Smiley, try something else ...
}
```

If the object pointed to by the argument of **dynamic_cast** (here, **ps**) is not of the expected type (here, **Smiley**) or a class derived from the expected type, **dynamic_cast** returns **nullptr**.

We use **dynamic_cast** to a pointer type when a pointer to an object of a different derived class is a valid argument. We then test whether the result is **nullptr**. This test can often conveniently be placed in the initialization of a variable in a condition.

When a different type is unacceptable, we can simply **dynamic_cast** to a reference type. If the object is not of the expected type, **bad_cast** is thrown:

```
Shape∗ ps {read_shape(cin)};
Smiley& r {dynamic_cast<Smiley&>(∗ps)};     // somewhere, catch std::bad_cast
```

Code is cleaner when **dynamic_cast** is used with restraint. If we can avoid using type information, we can write simpler and more efficient code, but occasionally type information is lost and must be recovered. This typically happens when we pass an object to some system that accepts an interface specified by a base class. When that system later passes the object back to use, we might have to recover the original type. Operations similar to **dynamic_cast** are known as "is kind of" and "is instance of" operations.

4.5.4 Avoiding Resource Leaks

Experienced programmers will notice that I left open two obvious opportunities for mistakes:
- A user might fail to **delete** the pointer returned by **read_shape()**.
- The owner of a container of **Shape** pointers might not **delete** the objects pointed to.

In that sense, functions returning a pointer to an object allocated on the free store are dangerous.

One solution to both problems is to return a standard-library **unique_ptr** (§11.2.1) rather than a "naked pointer" and store **unique_ptrs** in the container:

```
unique_ptr<Shape> read_shape(istream& is) // read shape descriptions from input stream is
{
    // read shape header from is and find its Kind k

    switch (k) {
    case Kind::circle:
        // read circle data {Point,int} into p and r
        return unique_ptr<Shape>{new Circle{p,r}};         // §11.2.1
    // ...
}

void user()
{
    vector<unique_ptr<Shape>> v;
    while (cin)
        v.push_back(read_shape(cin));
    draw_all(v);                    // call draw() for each element
    rotate_all(v,45);               // call rotate(45) for each element
} // all Shapes implicitly destroyed
```

Now the object is owned by the **unique_ptr** which will **delete** the object when it is no longer needed, that is, when its **unique_ptr** goes out of scope.

For the **unique_ptr** version of **user()** to work, we need versions of **draw_all()** and **rotate_all()** that accept **vector<unique_ptr<Shape>>**s. Writing many such **_all()** functions could become tedious, so §5.5 shows an alternative.

4.6 Copy and Move

By default, objects can be copied. This is true for objects of user-defined types as well as for built-in types. The default meaning of copy is memberwise copy: copy each member. For example, using **complex** from §4.2.1:

```
void test(complex z1)
{
    complex z2 {z1};        // copy initialization
    complex z3;
    z3 = z2;                // copy assignment
    // ...
}
```

Now **z1**, **z2**, and **z3** have the same value because both the assignment and the initialization copied both members.

When we design a class, we must always consider if and how an object might be copied. For simple concrete types, memberwise copy is often exactly the right semantics for copy. For some sophisticated concrete types, such as **Vector**, memberwise copy is not the right semantics for copy, and for abstract types it almost never is.

4.6.1 Copying Containers

When a class is a *resource handle* – that is, when the class is responsible for an object accessed through a pointer – the default memberwise copy is typically a disaster. Memberwise copy would violate the resource handle's invariant (§3.4.2). For example, the default copy would leave a copy of a **Vector** referring to the same elements as the original:

```
void bad_copy(Vector v1)
{
    Vector v2 = v1;        // copy v1's representation into v2
    v1[0] = 2;             // v2[0] is now also 2!
    v2[1] = 3;             // v1[1] is now also 3!
}
```

Assuming that **v1** has four elements, the result can be represented graphically like this:

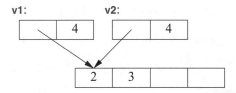

Fortunately, the fact that **Vector** has a destructor is a strong hint that the default (memberwise) copy semantics is wrong and the compiler should at least warn against this example. We need to define better copy semantics.

Copying of an object of a class is defined by two members: a *copy constructor* and a *copy assignment*:

```
class Vector {
private:
    double* elem;  // elem points to an array of sz doubles
    int sz;
public:
    Vector(int s);                          // constructor: establish invariant, acquire resources
    ~Vector() { delete[] elem; }            // destructor: release resources

    Vector(const Vector& a);                // copy constructor
    Vector& operator=(const Vector& a);     // copy assignment

    double& operator[](int i);
    const double& operator[](int i) const;

    int size() const;
};
```

A suitable definition of a copy constructor for **Vector** allocates the space for the required number of elements and then copies the elements into it, so that after a copy each **Vector** has its own copy of the elements:

```
Vector::Vector(const Vector& a)      // copy constructor
    :elem{new double[a.sz]},         // allocate space for elements
     sz{a.sz}
{
    for (int i=0; i!=sz; ++i)         // copy elements
        elem[i] = a.elem[i];
}
```

The result of the **v2=v1** example can now be presented as:

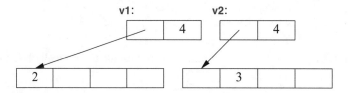

Of course, we need a copy assignment in addition to the copy constructor:

```
Vector& Vector::operator=(const Vector& a)       // copy assignment
{
    double* p = new double[a.sz];
    for (int i=0; i!=a.sz; ++i)
        p[i] = a.elem[i];
    delete[] elem;          // delete old elements
    elem = p;
    sz = a.sz;
    return *this;
}
```

The name **this** is predefined in a member function and points to the object for which the member function is called.

4.6.2 Moving Containers

We can control copying by defining a copy constructor and a copy assignment, but copying can be costly for large containers. We avoid the cost of copying when we pass objects to a function by using references, but we can't return a reference to a local object as the result (the local object would be destroyed by the time the caller got a chance to look at it). Consider:

```
Vector operator+(const Vector& a, const Vector& b)
{
    if (a.size()!=b.size())
        throw Vector_size_mismatch{};

    Vector res(a.size());
    for (int i=0; i!=a.size(); ++i)
        res[i]=a[i]+b[i];
    return res;
}
```

Returning from a **+** involves copying the result out of the local variable **res** and into some place where the caller can access it. We might use this **+** like this:

```
void f(const Vector& x, const Vector& y, const Vector& z)
{
    Vector r;
    // ...
    r = x+y+z;
    // ...
}
```

That would be copying a **Vector** at least twice (one for each use of the **+** operator). If a **Vector** is large, say, 10,000 **doubles**, that could be embarrassing. The most embarrassing part is that **res** in **operator+()** is never used again after the copy. We didn't really want a copy; we just wanted to get the result out of a function: we wanted to *move* a **Vector** rather than to *copy* it. Fortunately, we can state that intent:

```
class Vector {
    // ...

    Vector(const Vector& a);              // copy constructor
    Vector& operator=(const Vector& a);   // copy assignment

    Vector(Vector&& a);                   // move constructor
    Vector& operator=(Vector&& a);        // move assignment
};
```

Given that definition, the compiler will choose the *move constructor* to implement the transfer of the return value out of the function. This means that **r=x+y+z** will involve no copying of **Vector**s. Instead, **Vector**s are just moved.

As is typical, **Vector**'s move constructor is trivial to define:

```
Vector::Vector(Vector&& a)
    :elem{a.elem},          // "grab the elements" from a
     sz{a.sz}
{
    a.elem = nullptr;       // now a has no elements
    a.sz = 0;
}
```

The **&&** means "rvalue reference" and is a reference to which we can bind an rvalue. The word "rvalue" is intended to complement "lvalue," which roughly means "something that can appear on the left-hand side of an assignment." So an rvalue is – to a first approximation – a value that you can't assign to, such as an integer returned by a function call. Thus, an rvalue reference is a reference to something that *nobody else* can assign to, so that we can safely "steal" its value. The **res** local variable in **operator+()** for **Vector**s is an example.

A move constructor does *not* take a **const** argument: after all, a move constructor is supposed to remove the value from its argument. A *move assignment* is defined similarly.

A move operation is applied when an rvalue reference is used as an initializer or as the right-hand side of an assignment.

After a move, a moved-from object should be in a state that allows a destructor to be run. Typically, we should also allow assignment to a moved-from object.

Where the programmer knows that a value will not be used again, but the compiler can't be expected to be smart enough to figure that out, the programmer can be specific:

```
Vector f()
{
    Vector x(1000);
    Vector y(1000);
    Vector z(1000);
    z = x;                // we get a copy
    y = std::move(x);     // we get a move
    return z;             // we get a move
}
```

The standard-library function **move()** doesn't actually move anything. Instead, it returns a reference to its argument from which we may move – an *rvalue reference*.

Just before the **return** we have:

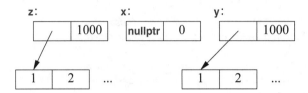

When **z** is destroyed, it too has been moved from (by the **return**) so that, like **x**, it is empty (it holds no elements).

4.6.3 Essential Operations

Construction of objects plays a key role in many designs. This wide variety of uses is reflected in the range and flexibility of the language features supporting initialization.

Constructors, destructors, and copy and move operations for a type are not logically separate. We must define them as a matched set or suffer logical or performance problems. If a class **X** has a destructor that performs a nontrivial task, such as free-store deallocation or lock release, the class is likely to need the full complement of functions:

```
class X {
public:
    X(Sometype);          // "ordinary constructor": create an object
    X();                  // default constructor
    X(const X&);          // copy constructor
    X(X&&);               // move constructor
    X& operator=(const X&); // copy assignment: clean up target and copy
    X& operator=(X&&);    // move assignment: clean up target and move
    ~X();                 // destructor: clean up
    // ...
};
```

There are five situations in which an object is copied or moved:
- As the source of an assignment
- As an object initializer
- As a function argument
- As a function return value
- As an exception

Except for assignment, a copy or move constructor will be used (unless it can be optimized away).

In addition to the initialization of named objects and objects on the free store, constructors are used to initialize temporary objects and to implement explicit type conversion.

Except for the "ordinary constructor," these special member functions will be generated by the compiler as needed. If you want to be explicit about generating default implementations, you can:

```
class Y {
public:
    Y(Sometype);
    Y(const Y&) = default;    // I really do want the default copy constructor
    Y(Y&&) = default;         // and the default move constructor
    // ...
};
```

If you are explicit about some defaults, other default definitions will not be generated.

When a class has a pointer or a reference member, it is usually a good idea to be explicit about copy and move operations. The reason is that a pointer or reference will point to something that the class needs to delete, in which case the default copy would be wrong, or it points to something that the class must not delete, in which case a reader of the code would like to know that.

A constructor taking a single argument defines a conversion from its argument type. For example, **complex** (§4.2.1) provides a constructor from a **double**:

```
complex z1 = 3.14;  // z1 becomes {3.14,0.0}
complex z2 = z1*2;  // z2 becomes {6.28,0.0}
```

This implicit conversion is sometimes ideal, but not always. For example, **Vector** (§4.2.2) provides a constructor from an **int**:

```
Vector v1 = 7;  // OK: v1 has 7 elements
```

This is typically considered unfortunate, and the standard-library **vector** does not allow this int-to-vector "conversion."

The way to avoid this problem is to say that only explicit "conversion" is allowed; that is, we can define the constructor like this:

```
class Vector {
public:
    explicit Vector(int s);    // no implicit conversion from int to Vector
    // ...
};
```

That gives us:

```
Vector v1(7);   // OK: v1 has 7 elements
Vector v2 = 7;  // error: no implicit conversion from int to Vector
```

When it comes to conversions, more types are like Vector than are like complex, so use explicit for constructors that take a single argument unless there is a good reason not to.

4.6.4 Resource Management

By defining constructors, copy operations, move operations, and a destructor, a programmer can provide complete control of the lifetime of a contained resource (such as the elements of a container). Furthermore, a move constructor allows an object to move simply and cheaply from one scope to another. That way, objects that we cannot or would not want to copy out of a scope can be simply and cheaply moved out instead. Consider a standard-library thread representing a concurrent activity (§13.2) and a Vector of a million doubles. We can't copy the former and don't want to copy the latter.

```
std::vector<thread> my_threads;

Vector init(int n)
{
    thread t {heartbeat};              // run heartbeat concurrently (on its own thread)
    my_threads.push_back(move(t));     // move t into my_threads
    // ... more initialization ...

    Vector vec(n);
    for (int i=0; i!=vec.size(); ++i)
        vec[i] = 777;
    return vec;                        // move vec out of init()
}

auto v = init(10000);      // start heartbeat and initialize v
```

Resource handles, such as Vector and thread, are superior alternatives to the use of pointers in many cases. In fact, the standard-library "smart pointers," such as unique_ptr, are themselves resource handles (§11.2.1).

I used the standard-library vector to hold the threads because we don't get to parameterize Vector with an element type until §5.2.

In very much the same way as new and delete disappear from application code, we can make pointers disappear into resource handles. In both cases, the result is simpler and more maintainable code, without added overhead. In particular, we can achieve *strong resource safety*; that is, we can eliminate resource leaks for a general notion of a resource. Examples are vectors holding memory, threads holding system threads, and fstreams holding file handles.

In many languages, resource management is primarily delegated to a garbage collector. C++ also offers a garbage collection interface so that you can plug in a garbage collector. However, I consider garbage collection the last alternative after cleaner, more general, and better localized alternatives to resource management have been exhausted.

Garbage collection is fundamentally a global memory management scheme. Clever implementations can compensate, but as systems are getting more distributed (think multicores, caches, and clusters), locality is more important than ever.

Also, memory is not the only resource. A resource is anything that has to be acquired and (explicitly or implicitly) released after use. Examples are memory, locks, sockets, file handles, and thread handles. A good resource management system handles all kinds of resources. Leaks must be avoided in any long-running systems, but excessive resource retention can be almost as bad as a leak. For example, if a system holds on to memory, locks, files, etc., for twice as long, the system needs to be provisioned with potentially twice as many resources.

Before resorting to garbage collection, systematically use resource handles: Let each resource have an owner in some scope and by default be released at the end of its owners scope. In C++, this is known as RAII (*Resource Acquisition Is Initialization*) and is integrated with error handling in the form of exceptions. Resources can be moved from scope to scope using move semantics or "smart pointers," and shared ownership can be represented by "shared pointers" (§11.2.1).

In the C++ standard library, RAII is pervasive: for example, memory (**string**, **vector**, **map**, **unordered_map**, etc.), files (**ifstream**, **ofstream**, etc.), threads (**thread**), locks (**lock_guard**, **unique_lock**, etc.), and general objects (through **unique_ptr** and **shared_ptr**). The result is implicit resource management that is invisible in common use and leads to low resource retention durations.

4.6.5 Suppressing Operations

Using the default copy or move for a class in a hierarchy is typically a disaster: given only a pointer to a base, we simply don't know what members the derived class has (§4.3), so we can't know how to copy them. So, the best thing to do is usually to *delete* the default copy and move operations, that is, to eliminate the default definitions of those two operations:

```
class Shape {
public:
        Shape(const Shape&) =delete;              // no copy operations
        Shape& operator=(const Shape&) =delete;

        Shape(Shape&&) =delete;                   // no move operations
        Shape& operator=(Shape&&) =delete;

        virtual ˜Shape();
        // ...
};
```

Now an attempt to copy a **Shape** will be caught by the compiler. If you need to copy an object in a class hierarchy, write a **virtual** clone function.

In this particular case, if you forgot to **delete** a copy or move operation, no harm is done. A move operation is *not* implicitly generated for a class where the user has explicitly declared a destructor, so you get a compiler error if you try to move a **Shape**. Furthermore, the generation of copy operations is deprecated in this case (§14.2.3), so you should expect the compiler to issue a warning if you try to copy a **Shape**.

A base class in a class hierarchy is just one example of an object we wouldn't want to copy. A resource handle generally cannot be copied just by copying its members (§4.6.1).

The **=delete** mechanism is general, that is, it can be used to suppress any operation.

4.7 Advice

[1]   The material in this chapter roughly corresponds to what is described in much greater detail in Chapters 16-22 of [Stroustrup,2013].

[2]   Express ideas directly in code; §4.1.

[3]   A concrete type is the simplest kind of class. Where applicable, prefer a concrete type over more complicated classes and over plain data structures; §4.2.

[4]   Use concrete classes to represent simple concepts and performance-critical components; §4.2.

[5]   Define a constructor to handle initialization of objects; §4.2.1, §4.6.3.

[6]   Make a function a member only if it needs direct access to the representation of a class; §4.2.1.

[7]   Define operators primarily to mimic conventional usage; §4.2.1.

[8]   Use nonmember functions for symmetric operators; §4.2.1.

[9]   Declare a member function that does not modify the state of its object const; §4.2.1.

[10] If a constructor acquires a resource, its class needs a destructor to release the resource; §4.2.2.

[11] Avoid "naked" new and delete operations; §4.2.2.

[12] Use resource handles and RAII to manage resources; §4.2.2.

[13] If a class is a container, give it an initializer-list constructor; §4.2.3.

[14] Use abstract classes as interfaces when complete separation of interface and implementation is needed; §4.3.

[15] Access polymorphic objects through pointers and references; §4.3.

[16] An abstract class typically doesn't need a constructor; §4.3.

[17] Use class hierarchies to represent concepts with inherent hierarchical structure; §4.5.

[18] A class with a virtual function should have a virtual destructor; §4.5.

[19] Use override to make overriding explicit in large class hierarchies; §4.5.1.

[20] When designing a class hierarchy, distinguish between implementation inheritance and interface inheritance; §4.5.2.

[21] Use dynamic_cast where class hierarchy navigation is unavoidable; §4.5.3.

[22] Use dynamic_cast to a reference type when failure to find the required class is considered a failure; §4.5.3.

[23] Use dynamic_cast to a pointer type when failure to find the required class is considered a valid alternative; §4.5.3.

[24] Use unique_ptr or shared_ptr to avoid forgetting to delete objects created using new; §4.5.4.

[25] Redefine or prohibit copying if the default is not appropriate for a type; §4.6.1, §4.6.5.

[26] Return containers by value (relying on move for efficiency); §4.6.2.

[27] For large operands, use const reference argument types; §4.6.2.

[28] If a class has a destructor, it probably needs user-defined or deleted copy and move operations; §4.6.5.

[29] Control construction, copy, move, and destruction of objects; §4.6.3.

[30] Design constructors, assignments, and the destructor as a matched set of operations; §4.6.3.

[31] If a default constructor, assignment, or destructor is appropriate, let the compiler generate it (don't rewrite it yourself); §4.6.3.

[32] By default, declare single-argument constructors **explicit**; §4.6.3.
[33] If a class has a pointer or reference member, it probably needs a destructor and non-default copy operations; §4.6.3.
[34] Provide strong resource safety; that is, never leak anything that you think of as a resource; §4.6.4.
[35] If a class is a resource handle, it needs a constructor, a destructor, and non-default copy operations; §4.6.4.

5

Templates

Your quote here.
– B. Stroustrup

- Introduction
- Parameterized Types
- Function Templates
- Concepts and Generic Programming
- Function Objects
- Variadic Templates
- Aliases
- Template Compilation Model
- Advice

5.1 Introduction

Someone who wants a vector is unlikely always to want a vector of doubles. A vector is a general concept, independent of the notion of a floating-point number. Consequently, the element type of a vector ought to be represented independently. A *template* is a class or a function that we parameterize with a set of types or values. We use templates to represent concepts that are best understood as something very general from which we can generate specific types and functions by specifying arguments, such as the element type double.

5.2 Parameterized Types

We can generalize our vector-of-doubles type to a vector-of-anything type by making it a template and replacing the specific type double with a parameter. For example:

```
template<typename T>
class Vector {
private:
    T* elem;    // elem points to an array of sz elements of type T
    int sz;
public:
    explicit Vector(int s);       // constructor: establish invariant, acquire resources
    ~Vector() { delete[] elem; }  // destructor: release resources

    // ... copy and move operations ...

    T& operator[](int i);
    const T& operator[](int i) const;
    int size() const { return sz; }
};
```

The `template<typename T>` prefix makes `T` a parameter of the declaration it prefixes. It is C++'s version of the mathematical "for all T" or more precisely "for all types T." Using `class` to introduce a type parameter is equivalent to using `typename`, and in older code we often see `template<class T>` as the prefix.

The member functions might be defined similarly:

```
template<typename T>
Vector<T>::Vector(int s)
{
    if (s<0)
        throw Negative_size{};
    elem = new T[s];
    sz = s;
}


template<typename T>
const T& Vector<T>::operator[](int i) const
{
    if (i<0 || size()<=i)
        throw out_of_range{"Vector::operator[]"};
    return elem[i];
}
```

Given these definitions, we can define `Vector`s like this:

```
Vector<char> vc(200);        // vector of 200 characters
Vector<string> vs(17);       // vector of 17 strings
Vector<list<int>> vli(45);   // vector of 45 lists of integers
```

The `>>` in `Vector<list<int>>` terminates the nested template arguments; it is not a misplaced input operator. It is not (as in C++98) necessary to place a space between the two `>`s.

A template plus a set of template arguments is called an *instantiation*. Late in the compilation process, at *instantiation time*, code is generated for each instantiation used in a program. This can be the cause of delayed and poor error messages.

We can use **Vector**s like this:

```
void write(const Vector<string>& vs)          // Vector of some strings
{
    for (int i = 0; i!=vs.size(); ++i)
        cout << vs[i] << '\n';
}
```

To support the range-**for** loop for our **Vector**, we must define suitable **begin()** and **end()** functions:

```
template<typename T>
T* begin(Vector<T>& x)
{
    return x.size() ? &x[0] : nullptr;        // pointer to first element or nullptr
}

template<typename T>
T* end(Vector<T>& x)
{
    return begin(x)+x.size();                 // pointer to one-past-last element
}
```

Given those, we can write:

```
void f2(Vector<string>& vs)      // Vector of some strings
{
    for (auto& s : vs)
        cout << s << '\n';
}
```

Similarly, we can define lists, vectors, maps (that is, associative arrays), unordered maps (that is, hash tables), etc., as templates (Chapter 9).

Templates are a compile-time mechanism, so their use incurs no run-time overhead compared to hand-crafted code. In fact, the code generated for **Vector<double>** is identical to the code generated for the version of **Vector** from Chapter 4. Furthermore, the code generated for the standard-library **vector<double>** is likely to be better (because more effort has gone into its implementation).

In addition to type arguments, a template can take value arguments. For example:

```
template<typename T, int N>
struct Buffer {
    using value_type = T;
    constexpr int size() { return N; }
    T[N];
    // ...
};
```

The alias (**value_type**) and the **constexpr** function are provided to allow users (read-only) access to the template arguments.

Value arguments are useful in many contexts. For example, **Buffer** allows us to create arbitrarily sized buffers with no overheads from the use of free store (dynamic memory):

```
Buffer<char,1024> glob;  // global buffer of characters (statically allocated)

void fct()
{
        Buffer<int,10> buf;  // local buffer of integers (on the stack)
        // ...
}
```

A template value argument must be a constant expression.

5.3 Function Templates

Templates have many more uses than simply parameterizing a container with an element type. In particular, they are extensively used for parameterization of both types and algorithms in the standard library (§9.6, §10.6). For example, we can write a function that calculates the sum of the element values of any container like this:

```
template<typename Container, typename Value>
Value sum(const Container& c, Value v)
{
        for (auto x : c)
                v+=x;
        return v;
}
```

The Value template argument and the function argument v are there to allow the caller to specify the type and initial value of the accumulator (the variable in which to accumulate the sum):

```
void user(Vector<int>& vi, std::list<double>& ld, std::vector<complex<double>>& vc)
{
        int x = sum(vi,0);                          // the sum of a vector of ints (add ints)
        double d = sum(vi,0.0);                     // the sum of a vector of ints (add doubles)
        double dd = sum(ld,0.0);                    // the sum of a list of doubles
        auto z = sum(vc,complex<double>{0.0,0.0});  // the sum of a vector of complex<double>s
}
```

The point of adding ints in a double would be to gracefully handle a number larger than the largest int. Note how the types of the template arguments for sum<T,V> are deduced from the function arguments. Fortunately, we do not need to explicitly specify those types.

This sum() is a simplified version of the standard-library accumulate() (§12.3).

A function template can be a member function, but not a virtual member. The compiler would not know all instantiations of a such a template in a program so it could not generate a vtbl (§4.4).

5.4 Concepts and Generic Programming

What are templates for? In other words, what programming techniques are effective when you use templates? Templates offer:

- The ability to pass types (as well as values and templates) as arguments without loss of information. This implies excellent opportunities for inlining, of which current implementations take great advantage.
- Delayed type checking (done at instantiation time). This implies opportunities to weave together information from different contexts.
- The ability to pass constant values as arguments. This implies the ability to do compile-time computation.

In other words, templates provide a powerful mechanism for compile-time computation and type manipulation that can lead to very compact and efficient code. Remember that types (classes) can contain both code and values.

The first and most common use of templates is to support *generic programming*, that is, programming focused on the design, implementation, and use of general algorithms. Here, "general" means that an algorithm can be designed to accept a wide variety of types as long as they meet the algorithm's requirements on its arguments. The template is C++'s main support for generic programming. Templates provide (compile-time) parametric polymorphism.

Consider the sum() from §5.3. It can be invoked for any data structure that supports begin() and end() so that the range-for will work. Such structures include the standard-library vector, list, and map. Furthermore, the element type of the data structure is limited only by its use: it must be a type that we can add to the Value argument. Examples are ints, doubles, and Matrixes (for any reasonable definition of Matrix). We could say that the sum() algorithm is generic in two dimensions: the type of the data structure used to store elements ("the container") and the type of elements.

So, sum() requires that its first template argument is some kind of container and its second template argument is some kind of number. We call such requirements *concepts*. Unfortunately, concepts cannot be expressed directly in C++11. All we can say is that the template argument for sum() must be types. There are techniques for checking concepts and proposals for direct language support for concepts [Stroustrup,2013] [Sutton,2011], but both are beyond the scope of this thin book.

Good, useful concepts are fundamental and are discovered more than they are designed. Examples are integer and floating-point number (as defined even in Classic C), more general mathematical concepts such as field and vector space, and container. They represent the fundamental concepts of a field of application. Identifying and formalizing to the degree necessary for effective generic programming can be a challenge.

For basic use, consider the concept *Regular*. A type is regular when it behaves much like an int or a vector. An object of a regular type

- can be default constructed.
- can be copied (with the usual semantics of copy yielding two objects that are independent and compare equal) using a constructor or an assignment.
- can be compared using == and !=.
- doesn't suffer technical problems from overly clever programming tricks.

A string is another example of a regular type. Like int, string is also *Ordered*. That is, two strings can be compared using <, <=, >, and >= with the appropriate semantics. Concepts is not just a syntactic notion, it is fundamentally about semantics. For example, don't define + to divide; that would not match the requirements for any reasonable number.

5.5   Function Objects

One particularly useful kind of template is the *function object* (sometimes called a *functor*), which is used to define objects that can be called like functions. For example:

```
template<typename T>
class Less_than {
    const T val;     // value to compare against
public:
    Less_than(const T& v) :val(v) { }
    bool operator()(const T& x) const { return x<val; } // call operator
};
```

The function called operator() implements the "function call," "call," or "application" operator (). We can define named variables of type Less_than for some argument type:

```
Less_than<int> lti {42};           // lti(i) will compare i to 42 using < (i<42)
Less_than<string> lts {"Backus"};  // lts(s) will compare s to "Backus" using < (s<"Backus")
```

We can call such an object, just as we call a function:

```
void fct(int n, const string & s)
{
    bool b1 = lti(n);    // true if n<42
    bool b2 = lts(s);    // true if s<"Backus"
    // ...
}
```

Such function objects are widely used as arguments to algorithms. For example, we can count the occurrences of values for which a predicate returns true:

```
template<typename C, typename P>
int count(const C& c, P pred)
{
    int cnt = 0;
    for (const auto& x : c)
        if (pred(x))
                ++cnt;
    return cnt;
}
```

A *predicate* is something that we can invoke to return true or false. For example:

```
void f(const Vector<int>& vec, const list<string>& lst, int x, const string& s)
{
    cout << "number of values less than " << x
        << ": " << count(vec,Less_than<int>{x})
        << '\n';
    cout << "number of values less than " << s
        << ": " << count(lst,Less_than<string>{s})
        << '\n';
}
```

Here, Less_than<int>{x} constructs an object for which the call operator compares to the int called x;

Less_than<string>{s} constructs an object that compares to the **string** called **s**. The beauty of these function objects is that they carry the value to be compared against with them. We don't have to write a separate function for each value (and each type), and we don't have to introduce nasty global variables to hold values. Also, for a simple function object like **Less_than** inlining is simple, so that a call of **Less_than** is far more efficient than an indirect function call. The ability to carry data plus their efficiency make function objects particularly useful as arguments to algorithms.

Function objects used to specify the meaning of key operations of a general algorithm (such as **Less_than** for **count()**) are often referred to as *policy objects*.

We have to define **Less_than** separately from its use. That could be seen as inconvenient. Consequently, there is a notation for implicitly generating function objects:

```
void f(const Vector<int>& vec, const list<string>& lst, int x, const string& s)
{
    cout << "number of values less than " << x
        << ": " << count(vec,[&](int a){ return a<x; })
        << '\n';
    cout << "number of values less than " << s
        << ": " << count(lst,[&](const string& a){ return a<s; })
        << '\n';
}
```

The notation **[&](int a){ return a<x; }** is called a *lambda expression*. It generates a function object exactly like **Less_than<int>{x}**. The **[&]** is a *capture list* specifying that local names used (such as **x**) will be accessed through references. Had we wanted to "capture" only **x**, we could have said so: **[&x]**. Had we wanted to give the generated object a copy of **x**, we could have said so: **[=x]**. Capture nothing is **[ ]**, capture all local names used by reference is **[&]**, and capture all local names used by value is **[=]**.

Using lambdas can be convenient and terse, but also obscure. For nontrivial actions (say, more than a simple expression), I prefer to name the operation so as to more clearly state its purpose and to make it available for use in several places in a program.

In §4.5.4, we noted the annoyance of having to write many functions to perform operations on elements of **vectors** of pointers and **unique_ptrs**, such as **draw_all()** and **rotate_all()**. Function objects (in particular, lambdas) can help by allowing us to separate the traversal of the container from the specification of what is to be done with each element.

First, we need a function that applies an operation to each object pointed to by the elements of a container of pointers:

```
template<typename C, typename Oper>
void for_all(C& c, Oper op)           // assume that C is a container of pointers
{
    for (auto& x : c)
        op(*x);           // pass op() a reference to each element pointed to
}
```

Now, we can write a version of **user()** from §4.5 without writing a set of _all functions:

```
void user()
{
    vector<unique_ptr<Shape>> v;
    while (cin)
        v.push_back(read_shape(cin));
    for_all(v,[](Shape& s){ s.draw(); });       // draw_all()
    for_all(v,[](Shape& s){ s.rotate(45); });   // rotate_all(45)
}
```

I pass a reference to Shape to a lambda so that the lambda doesn't have to care exactly how the objects are stored in the container. In particular, those for_all() calls would still work if I changed v to a vector<Shape∗>.

5.6 Variadic Templates

A template can be defined to accept an arbitrary number of arguments of arbitrary types. Such a template is called a *variadic template*. For example:

```
void f() { }        // do nothing

template<typename T, typename... Tail>
void f(T head, Tail... tail)
{
    g(head);   // do something to head
    f(tail...);   // try again with tail
}
```

The key to implementing a variadic template is to note that when you pass a list of arguments to it, you can separate the first argument from the rest. Here, we do something to the first argument (the head) and then recursively call f() with the rest of the arguments (the tail). The ellipsis, ..., is used to indicate "the rest" of a list. Eventually, of course, tail will become empty and we need a separate function to deal with that.

We can call this f() like this:

```
int main()
{
    cout << "first: ";
    f(1,2.2,"hello");

    cout << "\nsecond: ";
    f(0.2,'c',"yuck!",0,1,2);
    cout << "\n";
}
```

This would call f(1,2.2,"hello"), which will call f(2.2,"hello"), which will call f("hello"), which will call f(). What might the call g(head) do? Obviously, in a real program it will do whatever we wanted done to each argument. For example, we could make it write its argument (here, head) to output:

```
template<typename T>
void g(T x)
{
    cout << x << " ";
}
```

Given that, the output will be:

```
first: 1 2.2 hello
second: 0.2 c yuck! 0 1 2
```

It seems that f() is a simple variant of printf() printing arbitrary lists or values – implemented in three lines of code plus their surrounding declarations.

The strength of variadic templates (sometimes just called *variadics*) is that they can accept any arguments you care to give them. The weakness is that the type checking of the interface is a possibly elaborate template program.

Because of their flexibility, variadic templates are widely used in the standard library.

5.7 Aliases

Surprisingly often, it is useful to introduce a synonym for a type or a template. For example, the standard header <cstddef> contains a definition of the alias size_t, maybe:

```
using size_t = unsigned int;
```

The actual type named size_t is implementation-dependent, so in another implementation size_t may be an unsigned long. Having the alias size_t allows the programmer to write portable code.

It is very common for a parameterized type to provide an alias for types related to their template arguments. For example:

```
template<typename T>
class Vector {
public:
    using value_type = T;
    // ...
};
```

In fact, every standard-library container provides value_type as the name of its value type (Chapter 9). This allows us to write code that will work for every container that follows this convention. For example:

```
template<typename C>
using Element_type = typename C::value_type;    // the type of C's elements

template<typename Container>
void algo(Container& c)
{
    Vector<Element_type<Container>> vec;        // keep results here
    // ...
}
```

The aliasing mechanism can be used to define a new template by binding some or all template arguments. For example:

```
template<typename Key, typename Value>
class Map {
    // ...
};

template<typename Value>
using String_map = Map<string,Value>;

String_map<int> m;        // m is a Map<string,int>
```

5.8   Template Compilation Model

The type checking provided for templates checks the use of arguments in the template definition rather than against an explicit interface (in a template declaration). This provides a compile-time variant of what is often called *duck typing* ("If it walks like a duck and it quacks like a duck, it's a duck"). Or – using more technical terminology – we operate on values, and the presence and meaning of an operation depend solely on its operand values. This differs from the alternative view that objects have types, which determine the presence and meaning of operations. Values "live" in objects. This is the way objects (e.g., variables) work in C++, and only values that meet an object's requirements can be put into it. What is done at compile time using templates does not involve objects, only values.

The practical effect of this is that to use a template, its definition (not just its declaration) must be in scope. For example, the standard header **<vector>** holds the definition of **vector**. An unfortunate side effect is that a type error can be found uncomfortably late in the compilation process and can yield spectacularly bad error messages because the compiler found the problem by combining information from several places in the program.

5.9   Advice

[1]   The material in this chapter roughly corresponds to what is described in much greater detail in Chapters 20-29 of [Stroustrup,2013].
[2]   Use templates to express algorithms that apply to many argument types; §5.1.
[3]   Use templates to express containers; §5.2.
[4]   Use templates to raise the level of abstraction of code; §5.2.
[5]   When defining a template, first design and debug a non-template version; later generalize by adding parameters.
[6]   Templates are type-safe, but checking happens too late; §5.4.
[7]   A template can pass argument types without loss of information.
[8]   Use function templates to deduce class template argument types; §5.3.
[9]   Templates provide a general mechanism for compile-time programming; §5.4.

[10] When designing a template, carefully consider the concepts (requirements) assumed for its template arguments; §5.4.

[11] Use concepts as a design tool; §5.4.

[12] Use function objects as arguments to algoritms; §5.5.

[13] Use a lambda if you need a simple function object in one place only; §5.5.

[14] A virtual function member cannot be a template member function; §5.3.

[15] Use template aliases to simplify notation and hide implementation details; §5.7.

[16] Use variadic templates when you need a function that takes a variable number of arguments of a variety of types; §5.6.

[17] Don't use variadic templates for homogeneous argument lists (prefer initializer lists for that); §5.6.

[18] To use a template, make sure its definition (not just its declaration) is in scope; §5.8.

[19] Templates offer compile-time "duck typing"; §5.8.

[20] There is no separate compilation of templates: `#include` template definitions in every translation unit that uses them.

6

Library Overview

Why waste time learning
when ignorance is instantaneous?
– Hobbes

- Introduction
- Standard-Library Components
- Standard-Library Headers and Namespace
- Advice

6.1 Introduction

No significant program is written in just a bare programming language. First, a set of libraries is developed. These then form the basis for further work. Most programs are tedious to write in the bare language, whereas just about any task can be rendered simple by the use of good libraries.

Continuing from Chapters 1-5, Chapters 6-13 give a quick tour of key standard-library facilities.

I very briefly present useful standard-library types, such as **string**, **ostream**, **vector**, **map**, **unique_ptr**, **thread**, **regex**, and **complex**, as well as the most common ways of using them. As in Chapters 1-5, you are strongly encouraged not to be distracted or discouraged by an incomplete understanding of details. The purpose of this chapter is to convey a basic understanding of the most useful library facilities.

The specification of the standard library is almost two thirds of the ISO C++ standard. Explore it, and prefer it to home-made alternatives. Much thought has gone into its design, more still into its implementations, and much effort will go into its maintenance and extension.

The standard-library facilities described in this book are part of every complete C++ implementation. In addition to the standard-library components, most implementations offer "graphical user interface" systems (GUIs), Web interfaces, database interfaces, etc. Similarly, most application-development environments provide "foundation libraries" for corporate or industrial "standard" development and/or execution environments. Here, I do not describe such systems and libraries.

The intent is to provide a self-contained description of C++ as defined by the standard and to keep the examples portable. Naturally, a programmer is encouraged to explore the more extensive facilities available on most systems.

6.2 Standard-Library Components

The facilities provided by the standard library can be classified like this:
- Run-time language support (e.g., for allocation and run-time type information).
- The C standard library (with very minor modifications to minimize violations of the type system).
- Strings (with support for international character sets and localization); see §7.2.
- Support for regular expression matching; see §7.3.
- I/O streams is an extensible framework for input and output to which users can add their own types, streams, buffering strategies, locales, and character sets.
- A framework of containers (such as **vector** and **map**) and algorithms (such as **find()**, **sort()**, and **merge()**); see Chapter 9 and Chapter 10. This framework, conventionally called the STL [Stepanov,1994], is extensible so users can add their own containers and algorithms.
- Support for numerical computation (such as standard mathematical functions, complex numbers, vectors with arithmetic operations, and random number generators); see §4.2.1 and Chapter 12.
- Support for concurrent programming, including **threads** and locks; see Chapter 13. The concurrency support is foundational so that users can add support for new models of concurrency as libraries.
- Utilities to support template metaprogramming (e.g., type traits; §11.6), STL-style generic programming (e.g., **pair**; §11.3.3), and general programming (e.g., **clock**; §11.4).
- "Smart pointers" for resource management (e.g., **unique_ptr** and **shared_ptr**; §11.2.1) and an interface to garbage collectors (§4.6.4).
- Special-purpose containers, such as **array** (§11.3.1), **bitset** (§11.3.2), and **tuple** (§11.3.3).

The main criteria for including a class in the library were that:
- it could be helpful to almost every C++ programmer (both novices and experts),
- it could be provided in a general form that did not add significant overhead compared to a simpler version of the same facility, and
- that simple uses should be easy to learn (relative to the inherent complexity of their task).

Essentially, the C++ standard library provides the most common fundamental data structures together with the fundamental algorithms used on them.

6.3 Standard-Library Headers and Namespace

Every standard-library facility is provided through some standard header. For example:

```
#include<string>
#include<list>
```

This makes the standard **string** and **list** available.

The standard library is defined in a namespace (§3.3) called std. To use standard library facilities, the std:: prefix can be used:

```
std::string s {"Four legs Good; two legs Baaad!"};
std::list<std::string> slogans {"War is Peace", "Freedom is Slavery", "Ignorance is Strength"};
```

For simplicity, I will rarely use the std:: prefix explicitly in examples. Neither will I always #include the necessary headers explicitly. To compile and run the program fragments here, you must #include the appropriate headers and make the names they declare accessible. For example:

```
#include<string>           // make the standard string facilities accessible
using namespace std;       // make std names available without std:: prefix

string s {"C++ is a general–purpose programming language"};   // OK: string is std::string
```

It is generally in poor taste to dump every name from a namespace into the global namespace. However, in this book, I use the standard library exclusively and it is good to know what it offers.

Here is a selection of standard-library headers, all supplying declarations in namespace std:

Selected Standard Library Headers			
<algorithm>	copy(), find(), sort()	Chapter 10	§iso.25
<array>	array	§11.3.1	§iso.23.3.2
<chrono>	duration, time_point	§11.4	§iso.20.11.2
<cmath>	sqrt(), pow()	§12.2	§iso.26.8
<complex>	complex, sqrt(), pow()	§12.4	§iso.26.8
<forward_list>	forward_list	§9.6	§iso.23.3.4
<fstream>	fstream, ifstream, ofstream	§8.7	§iso.27.9.1
<future>	future, promise	§13.7	§iso.30.6
<ios>	hex, dec, scientific, fixed, defaultfloat	§8.6	§iso.27.5
<iostream>	istream, ostream, cin, cout	Chapter 8	§iso.27.4
<map>	map, multimap	§9.5	§iso.23.4.4
<memory>	unique_ptr, shared_ptr, allocator	§11.2.1	§iso.20.6
<random>	default_random_engine, normal_distribution	§12.5	§iso.26.5
<regex>	regex, smatch	§7.3	§iso.28.8
<string>	string, basic_string	§7.2	§iso.21.3
<set>	set, multiset	§9.6	§iso.23.4.6
<sstream>	istringstream, ostringstream	§8.8	§iso.27.8
<stdexcept>	length_error, out_of_range, runtime_error	§3.4.1	§iso.19.2
<thread>	thread	§13.2	§iso.30.3
<unordered_map>	unordered_map, unordered_multimap	§9.5	§iso.23.5.4
<utility>	move(), swap(), pair	Chapter 11	§iso.20.1
<vector>	vector	§9.2	§iso.23.3.6

This listing is far from complete.

Headers from the C standard library, such as <stdlib.h> are provided. For each such header there is also a version with its name prefixed by c and the .h removed. This version, such as <cstdlib> places its declarations in the std namespace.

6.4 Advice

[1]   The material in this chapter roughly corresponds to what is described in much greater detail in Chapter 30 of [Stroustrup,2013].

[2]   Don't reinvent the wheel; use libraries; §6.1.

[3]   When you have a choice, prefer the standard library over other libraries; §6.1.

[4]   Do not think that the standard library is ideal for everything; §6.1.

[5]   Remember to #include the headers for the facilities you use; §6.3.

[6]   Remember that standard-library facilities are defined in namespace std; §6.3.

7

Strings and Regular Expressions

Prefer the standard to the offbeat.
– Strunk & White

- Introduction
- Strings
    - **string** Implementation
- Regular Expressions
    - Searching; Regular Expression Notation; Iterators
- Advice

7.1 Introduction

Text manipulation is a major part of most programs. The C++ standard library offers a **string** type to save most users from C-style manipulation of arrays of characters through pointers. In addition, regular expression matching is offered to help find patterns in text. The regular expressions are provided in a form similar to what is common in most modern languages. Both **strings** and **regex** objects can use a variety of character types (e.g., Unicode).

7.2 Strings

The standard library provides a **string** type to complement the string literals (§1.3). The **string** type provides a variety of useful string operations, such as concatenation. For example:

```
string compose(const string& name, const string& domain)
{
    return name + '@' + domain;
}

auto addr = compose("dmr","bell–labs.com");
```

Here, addr is initialized to the character sequence dmr@bell–labs.com. "Addition" of strings means concatenation. You can concatenate a string, a string literal, a C-style string, or a character to a string. The standard string has a move constructor so returning even long strings by value is efficient (§4.6.2).

In many applications, the most common form of concatenation is adding something to the end of a string. This is directly supported by the += operation. For example:

```
void m2(string& s1, string& s2)
{
    s1 = s1 + '\n';   // append newline
    s2 += '\n';       // append newline
}
```

The two ways of adding to the end of a string are semantically equivalent, but I prefer the latter because it is more explicit about what it does, more concise, and possibly more efficient.

A string is mutable. In addition to = and +=, subscripting (using [ ]), and substring operations are supported. Among other useful features, it provides the ability to manipulate substrings. For example:

```
string name = "Niels Stroustrup";

void m3()
{
    string s = name.substr(6,10);       // s = "Stroustrup"
    name.replace(0,5,"nicholas");       // name becomes "nicholas Stroustrup"
    name[0] = toupper(name[0]);         // name becomes "Nicholas Stroustrup"
}
```

The substr() operation returns a string that is a copy of the substring indicated by its arguments. The first argument is an index into the string (a position), and the second is the length of the desired substring. Since indexing starts from 0, s gets the value Stroustrup.

The replace() operation replaces a substring with a value. In this case, the substring starting at 0 with length 5 is Niels; it is replaced by nicholas. Finally, I replace the initial character with its uppercase equivalent. Thus, the final value of name is Nicholas Stroustrup. Note that the replacement string need not be the same size as the substring that it is replacing.

Naturally, strings can be compared against each other and against string literals. For example:

```
string incantation;

void respond(const string& answer)
{
    if (answer == incantation) {
        // perform magic
    }
    else if (answer == "yes") {
        // ...
    }
    // ...
}
```

Among the many useful **string** operations are assignment (using **=**), subscripting (using **[ ]** or **at()** as for **vector**; §9.2.2), iteration (using iterators as for **vector**; §10.2), input (§8.3), streaming (§8.8).

If you need a C-style string (a zero-terminated array of **char**), **string** offers read-only access to its contained characters. For example:

```
void print(const string& s)
{
    printf("For people who like printf: %s\n",s.c_str());
    cout << "For people who like streams: " << s << '\n';
}
```

7.2.1 string **Implementation**

Implementing a string class is a popular and useful exercise. However, for general-purpose use, our carefully crafted first attempts rarely match the standard **string** in convenience or performance. These days, **string** is usually implemented using the *short-string optimization*. That is, short string values are kept in the **string** object itself and only longer strings are placed on free store. Consider:

```
string s1 {"Annemarie"};            // short string
string s2 {"Annemarie Stroustrup"}; // long string
```

The memory layout will be something like:

When a **string**'s value changes from a short to a long string (and vice verse) its representation adjusts appropriately.

The actual performance of **strings** can depend critically on the run-time environment. In particular, in multi-threaded implementations, memory allocation can be relatively costly. Also, when lots of strings of differing lengths are used, memory fragmentation can result. These are the main reasons that the short-string optimization has become ubiquitous.

To handle multiple character sets, **string** is really an alias for a general template **basic_string** with the character type **char**:

```
template<typename Char>
class basic_string {
    // ... string of Char ...
};

using string = basic_string<char>
```

A user can define strings of arbitrary character types. For example, assuming we have a Japanese character type **Jchar**, we can write:

```
using Jstring = basic_string<Jchar>;
```

Now we can do all the usual string operations on **Jstring**, a string of Japanese characters. Similarly, we can handle Unicode string.

7.3 Regular Expressions

Regular expressions are a powerful tool for text processing. They provide a way to simply and tersely describe patterns in text (e.g., a U.S. postal code such as **TX 77845**, or an ISO-style date, such as **2009–06–07**) and to efficiently find such patterns in text. In **<regex>**, the standard library provides support for regular expressions in the form of the **std::regex** class and its supporting functions. To give a taste of the style of the **regex** library, let us define and print a pattern:

```
regex pat {R"(\w{2}\s*\d{5}(-\d{4})?)"};    // US postal code pattern: XXddddd-dddd and variants
```

People who have used regular expressions in just about any language will find **\w{2}\s∗\d{5}(–\d{4})?** familiar. It specifies a pattern starting with two letters **\w{2}** optionally followed by some space **\s∗** followed by five digits **\d{5}** and optionally followed by a dash and four digits **–\d{4}**. If you are not familiar with regular expressions, this may be a good time to learn about them ([Stroustrup,2009], [Maddock,2009], [Friedl,1997]).

To express the pattern, I use a *raw string literal* starting with **R"(** and terminated by **)"**. This allows backslashes and quotes to be used directly in the string. Raw strings are particularly suitable for regular expressions because they tend to contain a lot of backslashes. Had I used a conventional string, the pattern definition would have been:

```
regex pat {"\\w{2}\\s∗\\d{5}(–\\d{4})?"};    // U.S. postal code pattern
```

In **<regex>**, the standard library provides support for regular expressions:
- **regex_match()**: Match a regular expression against a string (of known size) (§7.3.2).
- **regex_search()**: Search for a string that matches a regular expression in an (arbitrarily long) stream of data (§7.3.1).
- **regex_replace()**: Search for strings that match a regular expression in an (arbitrarily long) stream of data and replace them.
- **regex_iterator**: Iterate over matches and submatches (§7.3.3).
- **regex_token_iterator**: Iterate over non-matches.

7.3.1 Searching

The simplest way of using a pattern is to search for it in a stream:

```
int lineno = 0;
for (string line; getline(cin,line); ) {          // read into line buffer
    ++lineno;
    smatch matches;                               // matched strings go here
    if (regex_search(line,matches,pat))           // search for pat in line
        cout << lineno << ": " << matches[0] << '\n';
}
```

The **regex_search(line,matches,pat)** searches the **line** for anything that matches the regular expression stored in **pat** and if it finds any matches, it stores them in **matches**. If no match was found, regex_search(line,matches,pat) returns **false**. The **matches** variable is of type **smatch**. The "s" stands for "sub" or "string," and an **smatch** is a **vector** of sub-matches of type **string**. The first element, here **matches[0]**, is the complete match. The result of a **regex_search()** is a collection of matches, typically represented as an **smatch**:

```
void use()
{
    ifstream in("file.txt");      // input file
    if (!in)                      // check that the file was opened
        cerr << "no file\n";

    regex pat {R"(\w{2}\s*\d{5}(-\d{4})?)"};   // U.S. postal code pattern

    int lineno = 0;
    for (string line; getline(in,line); ) {
        ++lineno;
        smatch matches;      // matched strings go here
        if (regex_search(line, matches, pat)) {
            cout << lineno << ": " << matches[0] << '\n';       // the complete match
            if (1<matches.size() && matches[1].matched)
                cout  << "\t: " << matches[1] << '\n';          // submatch
        }
    }
}
```

This function reads a file looking for U.S. postal codes, such as **TX77845** and **DC 20500-0001**. An **smatch** type is a container of regex results. Here, **matches[0]** is the whole pattern and **matches[1]** is the optional four-digit subpattern.

The regular expression syntax and semantics are designed so that regular expressions can be compiled into state machines for efficient execution [Cox,2007]. The **regex** type performs this compilation at run time.

7.3.2 Regular Expression Notation

The **regex** library can recognize several variants of the notation for regular expressions. Here, I use the default notation, a variant of the ECMA standard used for ECMAScript (more commonly known as JavaScript).

The syntax of regular expressions is based on characters with special meaning:

Regular Expression Special Characters			
.	Any single character (a "wildcard")	\	Next character has a special meaning
[	Begin character class	*	Zero or more (suffix operation)
]	End character class	+	One or more (suffix operation)
{	Begin count	?	Optional (zero or one) (suffix operation)
}	End count	|	Alternative (or)
(	Begin grouping	^	Start of line; negation
)	End grouping	$	End of line

For example, we can specify a line starting with zero or more **A**s followed by one or more **B**s followed by an optional **C** like this:

    ^A*B+C?$

Examples that match:

    AAAAAAAAAAAABBBBBBBBBC
    BC
    B

Examples that do not match:

    AAAAA   // no B
     AAAABC   // initial space
    AABBCC   // too many Cs

A part of a pattern is considered a subpattern (which can be extracted separately from an **smatch**) if it is enclosed in parentheses. For example:

    \d+-\d+   // no subpatterns
    \d+(-\d+)   // one subpattern
    (\d+)(-\d+) // two subpatterns

A pattern can be optional or repeated (the default is exactly once) by adding a suffix:

Repetition	
{ n }	Exactly n times
{ n, }	n or more times
{n,m}	At least n and at most m times
*	Zero or more, that is, {0,}
+	One or more, that is, {1,}
?	Optional (zero or one), that is {0,1}

For example:

    A{3}B{2,4}C*

Examples that match:

    AAABBC
    AAABBB

Examples that do not match:

    AABBC   // too few As
    AAABC   // too few Bs
    AAABBBBBCCC   // too many Bs

A suffix **?** after any of the repetition notations (**?**, *****, **+**, and **{ }**) makes the pattern matcher "lazy" or "non-greedy." That is, when looking for a pattern, it will look for the shortest match rather than the longest. By default, the pattern matcher always looks for the longest match; this is known as the *Max Munch rule*. Consider:

ababab

The pattern (ab)+ matches all of ababab. However, (ab)+? matches only the first ab.

The most common character classifications have names:

Character Classes	
alnum	Any alphanumeric character
alpha	Any alphabetic character
blank	Any whitespace character that is not a line separator
cntrl	Any control character
d	Any decimal digit
digit	Any decimal digit
graph	Any graphical character
lower	Any lowercase character
print	Any printable character
punct	Any punctuation character
s	Any whitespace character
space	Any whitespace character
upper	Any uppercase character
w	Any word character (alphanumeric characters plus the underscore)
xdigit	Any hexadecimal digit character

In a regular expression, a character class name must be bracketed by [: :]. For example, [:digit:] matches a decimal digit. Furthermore, they must be used within a [ ] pair defining a character class.

Several character classes are supported by shorthand notation:

Character Class Abbreviations		
\d	A decimal digit	[[:digit:]]
\s	A space (space, tab, etc.)	[[:space:]]
\w	A letter (a-z) or digit (0-9) or underscore (_)	[_[:alnum:]]
\D	Not \d	[^[:digit:]]
\S	Not \s	[^[:space:]]
\W	Not \w	[^_[:alnum:]]

In addition, languages supporting regular expressions often provide:

Nonstandard (but Common) Character Class Abbreviations		
\l	A lowercase character	[[:lower:]]
\u	An uppercase character	[[:upper:]]
\L	Not \l	[^[:lower:]]
\U	Not \u	[^[:upper:]]

For full portability, use the character class names rather than these abbreviations.

As an example, consider writing a pattern that describes C++ identifiers: an underscore or a letter followed by a possibly empty sequence of letters, digits, or underscores. To illustrate the subtleties involved, I include a few false attempts:

```
[:alpha:][:alnum:]*              // wrong: characters from the set ":alph" followed by ...
[[:alpha:]][[:alnum:]]*          // wrong: doesn't accept underscore ('_' is not alpha)
([[:alpha:]]|_)[[:alnum:]]*      // wrong: underscore is not part of alnum either

([[:alpha:]]|_)([[:alnum:]]|_)*  // OK, but clumsy
[[:alpha:]_][[:alnum:]_]*        // OK: include the underscore in the character classes
[_[:alpha:]][_[:alnum:]]*        // also OK
[_[:alpha:]]\w*                  // \w is equivalent to [_[:alnum:]]
```

Finally, here is a function that uses the simplest version of **regex_match()** (§7.3.1) to test whether a string is an identifier:

```
bool is_identifier(const string& s)
{
        regex pat {"[_[:alpha:]]\\w*"};  // underscore or letter
                                    // followed by zero or more underscores, letters, or digits
        return regex_match(s,pat);
}
```

Note the doubling of the backslash to include a backslash in an ordinary string literal. Use raw string literals to alleviate problems with special characters. For example:

```
bool is_identifier(const string& s)
{
        regex pat {R"([_[:alpha:]]\w*)"};
        return regex_match(s,pat);
}
```

Here are some examples of patterns:

```
Ax*              // A, Ax, Axxxx
Ax+              // Ax, Axxx      Not A
\d-?\d           // 1-2, 12       Not 1--2
\w{2}-\d{4,5}    // Ab-1234, XX-54321, 22-5432      Digits are in \w
(\d*:)?(\d+)     // 12:3, 1:23, 123, :123    Not 123:
(bs|BS)          // bs, BS        Not bS
[aeiouy]         // a, o, u       An English vowel, not x
[^aeiouy]        // x, k          Not an English vowel, not e
[a^eiouy]        // a, ^, o, u    An English vowel or ^
```

A **group** (a subpattern) potentially to be represented by a **sub_match** is delimited by parentheses. If you need parentheses that should not define a subpattern, use **(?:** rather than plain **(**. For example:

```
(\s|:|,)*(\d*)     // spaces, colons, and/or commas followed by a number
```

Assuming that we were not interested in the characters before the number (presumably separators), we could write:

```
(?:\s|:|,)*(\d*)   // spaces, colons, and/or commas followed by a number
```

This would save the regular expression engine from having to store the first characters: the **(?** variant has only one subpattern.

Regular Expression Grouping Examples	
\d*\s\w+	No groups (subpatterns)
(\d*)\s(\w+)	Two groups
(\d*)(\s(\w+))+	Two groups (groups do not nest)
(\s*\w*)+	One group; one or more subpatterns; only the last subpattern is saved as a **sub_match**
<(.*?)>(.*?)</\1>	Three groups; the \1 means "same as group 1"

That last pattern is useful for parsing XML. It finds tag/end-of-tag markers. Note that I used a non-greedy match (a *lazy match*), .*?, for the subpattern between the tag and the end tag. Had I used plain .*, this input would have caused a problem:

Always look for the bright side of life.

A *greedy match* for the first subpattern would match the first < with the last >. That would be correct behavior, but unlikely what the programmer wanted.

For a more exhaustive presentation of regular expressions, see [Friedl,1997].

7.3.3 Iterators

We can define a **regex_iterator** for iterating over a sequence of characters finding matches for a pattern. For example, we can use a **sregex_iterator**, (a **regex_iterator<string>**) to output all whitespace-separated words in a **string**:

```
void test()
{
    string input = "aa as; asd ++eˆasdf asdfg";
    regex pat {R"(\s+(\w+))"};
    for (sregex_iterator p(input.begin(),input.end(),pat); p!=sregex_iterator{}; ++p)
        cout << (*p)[1] << '\n';
}
```

This outputs:

```
as
asd
asdfg
```

We missed the first word, **aa**, because it has no preceding whitespace. If we simplify the pattern to R"((\w+))", we get

```
aa
as
asd
e
asdf
asdfg
```

A **regex_iterator** is a bidirectional iterator, so we cannot directly iterate over an **istream**. Also, we cannot write through a **regex_iterator**, and the default **regex_iterator** (**regex_iterator{}**) is the only possible end-of-sequence.

7.4 Advice

[1]   The material in this chapter roughly corresponds to what is described in much greater detail in Chapters 36-37 of [Stroustrup,2013].

[2]   Prefer **string** operations to C-style string functions; §7.1.

[3]   Use **string** to declare variables and members rather than as a base class; §7.2.

[4]   Return **strings** by value (rely on move semantics); §7.2, §7.2.1.

[5]   Directly or indirectly, use **substr()** to read substrings and **replace()** to write substrings; §7.2.

[6]   A **string** can grow and shrink, as needed; §7.2.

[7]   Use **at()** rather than iterators or **[ ]** when you want range checking; §7.2.

[8]   Use iterators and **[ ]** rather than **at()** when you want to optimize speed; §7.2.

[9]   **string** input doesn't overflow; §7.2, §8.3.

[10] Use **c_str()** to produce a C-style string representation of a **string** (only) when you have to; §7.2.

[11] Use a **string_stream** or a generic value extraction function (such as **to<X>**) for numeric conversion of strings; §8.8.

[12] A **basic_string** can be used to make strings of characters on any type; §7.2.1.

[13] Use **regex** for most conventional uses of regular expressions; §7.3.

[14] Prefer raw string literals for expressing all but the simplest patterns; §7.3.

[15] Use **regex_match()** to match a complete input; §7.3, §7.3.2.

[16] Use **regex_search()** to search for a pattern in an input stream; §7.3.1.

[17] The regular expression notation can be adjusted to match various standards; §7.3.2.

[18] The default regular expression notation is that of ECMAScript; §7.3.2.

[19] Be restrained; regular expressions can easily become a write-only language; §7.3.2.

[20] Note that \i allows you to express a subpattern in terms of a previous subpattern; §7.3.2.

[21] Use **?** to make patterns "lazy"; §7.3.2.

[22] Use **regex_iterators** for iterating over a stream looking for a pattern; §7.3.3

8

I/O Streams

What you see is all you get.
— Brian W. Kernighan

8.1 Introduction

The I/O stream library provides formatted and unformatted buffered I/O of text and numeric values.

An **ostream** converts typed objects to a stream of characters (bytes):

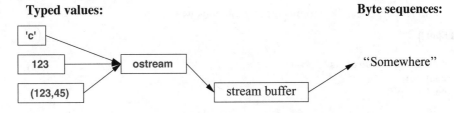

An **istream** converts a stream of characters (bytes) to typed objects:

Typed values: **Byte sequences:**

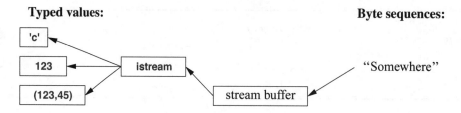

The operations on istreams and ostreams are described in §8.3 and §8.2. The operations are type-safe, type-sensitive, and extensible to handle user-defined types.

Other forms of user interaction, such as graphical I/O, are handled through libraries that are not part of the ISO standard and therefore not described here.

These streams can be used for binary I/O, be used for a variety of character types, be locale specific, and use advanced buffering strategies, but these topics are beyond the scope of this book.

8.2 Output

In <ostream>, the I/O stream library defines output for every built-in type. Further, it is easy to define output of a user-defined type (§8.5). The operator << ("put to") is used as an output operator on objects of type ostream; cout is the standard output stream and cerr is the standard stream for reporting errors. By default, values written to cout are converted to a sequence of characters. For example, to output the decimal number 10, we can write:

```
void f()
{
    cout << 10;
}
```

This places the character 1 followed by the character 0 on the standard output stream.

Equivalently, we could write:

```
void g()
{
    int i {10};
    cout << i;
}
```

Output of different types can be combined in the obvious way:

```
void h(int i)
{
    cout << "the value of i is ";
    cout << i;
    cout << '\n';
}
```

For h(10), the output will be:

the value of i is 10

People soon tire of repeating the name of the output stream when outputting several related items. Fortunately, the result of an output expression can itself be used for further output. For example:

```
void h2(int i)
{
    cout << "the value of i is " << i << '\n';
}
```

This h2() produces the same output as h().

A character constant is a character enclosed in single quotes. Note that a character is output as a character rather than as a numerical value. For example:

```
void k()
{
    int b = 'b';        // note: char implicitly converted to int
    char c = 'c';
    cout << 'a' << b << c;
}
```

The integer value of the character 'b' is 98 (in the ASCII encoding used on the C++ implementation that I used), so this will output a98c.

8.3 Input

In <istream>, the standard library offers istreams for input. Like ostreams, istreams deal with character string representations of built-in types and can easily be extended to cope with user-defined types.

The operator >> ("get from") is used as an input operator; cin is the standard input stream. The type of the right-hand operand of >> determines what input is accepted and what is the target of the input operation. For example:

```
void f()
{
    int i;
    cin >> i;           // read an integer into i

    double d;
    cin >> d;           // read a double-precision floating-point number into d
}
```

This reads a number, such as 1234, from the standard input into the integer variable i and a floating-point number, such as 12.34e5, into the double-precision floating-point variable d.

Like output operations, input operations can be chained, so I could equivalently have written:

```
void f()
{
    int i;
    double d;
    cin >> i >> d;        // read into i and d
}
```

In both cases, the read of the integer is terminated by any character that is not a digit. By default, >> skips initial whitespace, so a suitable complete input sequence would be

```
1234
12.34e5
```

Often, we want to read a sequence of characters. A convenient way of doing that is to read into a string. For example:

```
void hello()
{
    cout << "Please enter your name\n";
    string str;
    cin >> str;
    cout << "Hello, " << str << "!\n";
}
```

If you type in Eric the response is:

Hello, Eric!

By default, a whitespace character, such as a space or a newline, terminates the read, so if you enter Eric Bloodaxe pretending to be the ill-fated king of York, the response is still:

Hello, Eric!

You can read a whole line (including the terminating newline character) using the getline() function. For example:

```
void hello_line()
{
    cout << "Please enter your name\n";
    string str;
    getline(cin,str);
    cout << "Hello, " << str << "!\n";
}
```

With this program, the input Eric Bloodaxe yields the desired output:

Hello, Eric Bloodaxe!

The newline that terminated the line is discarded, so cin is ready for the next input line.

The standard strings have the nice property of expanding to hold what you put in them; you don't have to precalculate a maximum size. So, if you enter a couple of megabytes of semicolons, the program will echo pages of semicolons back at you.

8.4 I/O State

An iostream has a state that we can examine to determine whether an operation succeeded. The most common use is to read a sequence of values:

```
vector<int> read_ints(istream& is)
{
    vector<int> res;
    int i;
    while (is>>i)
        res.push_back(i);
    return res;
}
```

This reads from is until something that is not an integer is encountered. That something will typically be the end of input. What is happening here is that the operation is>>i returns a reference to is, and testing an iostream yields true if the stream is ready for another operation.

In general, the I/O state holds all the information needed to read or write, such as formatting information (§8.6), error state (e.g., has end-of-input been reached?), and what kind of buffering is used. In particular, a user can set the state to reflect that an error has occurred (§8.5) and clear the state if an error wasn't serious. For example, we could imagine reading a sequence of integers than might contain some form of nesting:

```
while (cin) {
    for (int i; cin>>i; ) {
        // ... use the integer ...
    }

    if (cin.eof()) {
        // .. all is well we reached the end-of-file ...
    }
    else if (cin.fail()) {          // a potentially recoverable error
        cin.clear();                // reset the state to good()
        char ch;
        if (cin>>ch) {              // look for nesting represented by { ... }
            switch (ch) {
            case '{':
                // ... start nested structure ...
                break;
            case '}':
                // ... end nested structure ...
                break;
            default:
                cin.setstate(ios_base::failbit);    // add fail() to cin's state
            }
        }
    }
    // ...
}
```

8.5 I/O of User-Defined Types

In addition to the I/O of built-in types and standard **strings**, the **iostream** library allows programmers to define I/O for their own types. For example, consider a simple type **Entry** that we might use to represent entries in a telephone book:

```
struct Entry {
    string name;
    int number;
};
```

We can define a simple output operator to write an **Entry** using a *{"name",number}* format similar to the one we use for initialization in code:

```
ostream& operator<<(ostream& os, const Entry& e)
{
    return os << "{\"" << e.name << "\", " << e.number << "}";
}
```

A user-defined output operator takes its output stream (by reference) as its first argument and returns it as its result.

The corresponding input operator is more complicated because it has to check for correct formatting and deal with errors:

```
istream& operator>>(istream& is, Entry& e)
    // read { "name" , number } pair. Note: formatted with { " " , and }
{
    char c, c2;
    if (is>>c && c=='{' && is>>c2 && c2=='"') { // start with a { "
        string name;                 // the default value of a string is the empty string: ""
        while (is.get(c) && c!='"')  // anything before a " is part of the name
            name+=c;

        if (is>>c && c==',') {
            int number = 0;
            if (is>>number>>c && c=='}') { // read the number and a }
                e = {name,number};      // assign to the entry
                return is;
            }
        }
    }
    is.setstate(ios_base::failbit);       // register the failure in the stream
    return is;
}
```

An input operation returns a reference to its **istream** which can be used to test if the operation succeeded. For example, when used as a condition, **is>>c** means "Did we succeed at reading from **is** into **c**?"

The **is>>c** skips whitespace by default, but **is.get(c)** does not, so that this **Entry**-input operator ignores (skips) whitespace outside the name string, but not within it. For example:

```
{ "John Marwood Cleese" , 123456        }
{"Michael Edward Palin",987654}
```

We can read such a pair of values from input into an **Entry** like this:

```
for (Entry ee; cin>>ee; )  // read from cin into ee
        cout << ee << '\n';  // write ee to cout
```

The output is:

```
{"John Marwood Cleese", 123456}
{"Michael Edward Palin", 987654}
```

See §7.3 for a more systematic technique for recognizing patterns in streams of characters (regular expression matching).

8.6 Formatting

The **iostream** library provides a large set of operations for controlling the format of input and output. The simplest formatting controls are called *manipulators* and are found in **<ios>**, **<istream>**, **<ostream>**, and **<iomanip>** (for manipulators that take arguments): For example, we can output integers as decimal (the default), octal, or hexadecimal numbers:

```
cout << 1234 << ',' << hex << 1234 << ',' << oct << 1234 << '\n';        // print 1234,4d2,2322
```

We can explicitly set the output format for floating-point numbers:

```
constexpr double d = 123.456;
```

```
cout << d << "; "                        // use the default format for d
        << scientific <<  d << "; "      // use 1.123e2 style format for d
        << hexfloat <<  d << "; "        // use hexadecimal notation for d
        << fixed << d << "; "            // use 123.456 style format for d
        << defaultfloat << d << '\n';    // use the default format for d
```

This produces:

```
123.456; 1.234560e+002; 0x1.edd2f2p+6; 123.456000; 123.456
```

Precision is an integer that determines the number of digits used to display a floating-point number:

- The *general* format (**defaultfloat**) lets the implementation choose a format that presents a value in the style that best preserves the value in the space available. The precision specifies the maximum number of digits.
- The *scientific* format (**scientific**) presents a value with one digit before a decimal point and an exponent. The precision specifies the maximum number of digits after the decimal point.
- The *fixed* format (**fixed**) presents a value as an integer part followed by a decimal point and a fractional part. The precision specifies the maximum number of digits after the decimal point.

Floating-point values are rounded rather than just truncated, and **precision()** doesn't affect integer output. For example:

```
cout.precision(8);
cout << 1234.56789 << ' ' << 1234.56789 << ' ' << 123456 << '\n';

cout.precision(4);
cout << 1234.56789 << ' ' << 1234.56789 << ' ' << 123456 << '\n';
```

This produces:

```
1234.5679 1234.5679 123456
1235 1235 123456
```

These manipulators are "sticky"; that is, it persists for subsequent floating-point operations.

8.7 File Streams

In <fstream>, the standard library provides streams to and from a file:
- ifstreams for reading from a file
- ofstreams for writing to a file
- fstreams for reading from and writing to a file

For example:

```
ofstream ofs {"target"};          // "o" for "output"
if (!ofs)
        error("couldn't open 'target' for writing");
```

Testing that a file stream has been properly opened is usually done by checking its state.

```
fstream ifs {"source"};          // "i" for "input"
if (!ifs)
        error("couldn't open 'source' for reading");
```

Assuming that the tests succeeded, ofs can be used as an ordinary ostream (just like cout) and ifs can be used as an ordinary istream (just like cin).

File positioning and more detailed control of the way a file is opened is possible, but beyond the scope of this book.

8.8 String Streams

In <sstream>, the standard library provides streams to and from a string:
- istringstreams for reading from a string
- ostringstreams for writing to a string
- stringstreams for reading from and writing to a string.

For example:

```
void test()
{
        ostringstream oss;
```

```
        oss << "{temperature," << scientific << 123.4567890 << "}";
        cout << oss.str() << '\n';
}
```

The result from an istringstream can be read using str(). One common use of an ostringstream is to format before giving the resulting string to a GUI. Similarly, a string received from a GUI can be read using formatted input operations (§8.3) by putting it into an istringstream.

A stringstream can be used for both reading and writing. For example, we can define an operation that can convert any type with a string representation to another that also has a string representation:

```
template<typename Target =string, typename Source =string>
Target to(Source arg)              // convert Source to Target
{
    stringstream interpreter;
    Target result;

    if (!(interpreter << arg)              // write arg into stream
        || !(interpreter >> result)        // read result from stream
        || !(interpreter >> std::ws).eof())  // stuff left in stream?
        throw runtime_error{"to<>() failed"};

    return result;
}
```

A function template argument needs to be explicitly mentioned only if it cannot be deduced or if there is no default, so we can write:

```
auto x1 = to<string,double>(1.2);    // very explicit (and verbose)
auto x2 = to<string>(1.2);           // Source is deduced to double
auto x3 = to<>(1.2);                 // Target is defaulted to string; Source is deduced to double
auto x4 = to(1.2);                   // the <> is redundant;
                                     // Target is defaulted to string; Source is deduced to double
```

If all function template arguments are defaulted, the <> can be left out.

I consider this a good example of the generality and ease of use that can be achieved by a combination of language features and standard-library facilities.

8.9 Advice

[1]   The material in this chapter roughly corresponds to what is described in much greater detail in Chapter 38 of [Stroustrup,2013].

[2]   iostreams are type-safe, type-sensitive, and extensible; §8.1.

[3]   Define << and >> for user-defined types with values that have meaningful textual representations; §8.1, §8.2, §8.3.

[4]   Use cout for normal output and cerr for errors; §8.1.

[5]   There are iostreams for ordinary characters and wide characters, and you can define an iostream for any kind of character; §8.1.

[6]   Binary I/O is supported; §8.1.
[7]   There are standard iostreams for standard I/O streams, files, and strings; §8.2, §8.3, §8.7, §8.8.
[8]   Chain << operations for a terser notation; §8.2.
[9]   Chain >> operations for a terser notation; §8.3.
[10]   Input into strings does not overflow; §8.3.
[11]   By default >> skips initial whitespace; §8.3.
[12]   Use the stream state fail to handle potentially recoverable I/O errors; §8.4.
[13]   You can define << and >> operators for your own types; §8.5.
[14]   You don't need to modify istream or ostream to add new << and >> operators; §8.5.
[15]   Use manipulators to control formatting; §8.6.
[16]   precision() specifications apply to all following floating-point output operations; §8.6.
[17]   Floating-point format specifications (e.g., scientific) apply to all following floating-point output operations; §8.6.
[18]   #include <ios> when using standard manipulators; §8.6.
[19]   #include <iomanip> when using standard manipulators taking arguments; §8.6.
[20]   Don't try to copy a file stream.
[21]   Remember to check that a file stream is attached to a file before using it; §8.7.
[22]   Use stringstreams for in-memory formatting; §8.8.
[23]   You can define conversions between any two types that both have string representation; §8.8.

9

Containers

It was new.
It was singular.
It was simple.
It must succeed!
– H. Nelson

9.1 Introduction

Most computing involves creating collections of values and then manipulating such collections. Reading characters into a **string** and printing out the **string** is a simple example. A class with the main purpose of holding objects is commonly called a *container*. Providing suitable containers for a given task and supporting them with useful fundamental operations are important steps in the construction of any program.

To illustrate the standard-library containers, consider a simple program for keeping names and telephone numbers. This is the kind of program for which different approaches appear "simple and obvious" to people of different backgrounds. The **Entry** class from §8.5 can be used to hold a simple phone book entry. Here, we deliberately ignore many real-world complexities, such as the fact that many phone numbers do not have a simple representation as a 32-bit **int**.

9.2   vector

The most useful standard-library container is vector. A vector is a sequence of elements of a given type. The elements are stored contiguously in memory. A typical implementation of vector (§4.2.2, §4.6) will consist of a handle holding pointers to the first element, one-past-the-last element, and one-past-the-last allocated space (§10.1) (or the equivalent information represented as a pointer plus offsets):

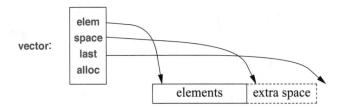

In addition, it holds an allocator (here, alloc), from which the vector can acquire memory for its elements. The default allocator uses new and delete to acquire and release memory.

We can initialize a vector with a set of values of its element type:

```
vector<Entry> phone_book = {
    {"David Hume",123456},
    {"Karl Popper",234567},
    {"Bertrand Arthur William Russell",345678}
};
```

Elements can be accessed through subscripting:

```
void print_book(const vector<Entry>& book)
{
    for (int i = 0; i!=book.size(); ++i)
        cout << book[i] << '\n';
}
```

As usual, indexing starts at 0 so that book[0] holds the entry for David Hume. The vector member function size() gives the number of elements.

The elements of a vector constitute a range, so we can use a range-for loop (§1.8):

```
void print_book(const vector<Entry>& book)
{
    for (const auto& x : book)      // for "auto" see §1.5
        cout << x << '\n';
}
```

When we define a vector, we give it an initial size (initial number of elements):

```
vector<int> v1 = {1, 2, 3, 4};      // size is 4
vector<string> v2;                  // size is 0
vector<Shape*> v3(23);              // size is 23; initial element value: nullptr
vector<double> v4(32,9.9);          // size is 32; initial element value: 9.9
```

An explicit size is enclosed in ordinary parentheses, for example, (23), and by default the elements are initialized to the element type's default value (e.g., **nullptr** for pointers and **0** for numbers). If you don't want the default value, you can specify one as a second argument (e.g., **9.9** for the **32** elements of **v4**).

The initial size can be changed. One of the most useful operations on a **vector** is push_back(), which adds a new element at the end of a **vector**, increasing its size by one. For example:

```
void input()
{
    for (Entry e; cin>>e; )
        phone_book.push_back(e);
}
```

This reads **Entrys** from the standard input into **phone_book** until either the end-of-input (e.g., the end of a file) is reached or the input operation encounters a format error.

The standard-library **vector** is implemented so that growing a **vector** by repeated push_back()s is efficient. To show how, consider an elaboration of the simple **Vector** from (Chapter 4 and Chapter 5) using the representation indicated in the diagram above:

```
template<typename T>
class Vector {
    T* elem;        // pointer to first element
    T* space;       // pointer to first unused (and uninitialized) slot
    T* last;        // pointer to last slot
public:
    // ...
    int size();                    // number of elements (space-elem)
    int capacity();                // number of slots available for elements (last-elem)
    // ...
    void reserve(int newsz);       // increase capacity() to newsz
    // ...
    void push_back(const T& t);    // copy t into Vector
    void push_back(T&& t);         // move t into Vector
};
```

The standard-libray **vector** has members **capacity()**, **reserve()**, and **push_back()**. The **reserve()** is used by users of **vector** and other **vector** members to make room for more elements. It may have to allocate new memory and when it does it moves the elements to the new allocation.

Given **capacity()** and **reserve()**, implementing **push_back()** is trivial:

```
template<typename T>
void Vector<T>::push_back(const T& t)
{
    if (capacity()<size()+1)              // make sure we have space for t
        reserve(size()==0?8:2*size()); // double the capacity
    new(space) T{t};                      // initialize *space to t
    ++space;
}
```

Now allocation and relocation of elements happens only infrequently. I used to use **reserve()** to try to improve performance, but that turned out to be a waste of effort: The heuristic used by **vector** is better than my guesses, so now I only use reserve() to avoid rellocation of elements when I want to use pointers to elements.

A vector can be copied in assignments and initializations. For example:

```
vector<Entry> book2 = phone_book;
```

Copying and moving of vectors are implemented by constructors and assignment operators as described in §4.6. Assigning a vector involves copying its elements. Thus, after the initialization of book2, book2 and phone_book hold separate copies of every Entry in the phone book. When a vector holds many elements, such innocent-looking assignments and initializations can be expensive. Where copying is undesirable, references or pointers (§1.8) or move operations (§4.6.2) should be used.

The standard-library vector is very flexible and efficient. Use it as your default container; that is, use it unless you have a solid reason to use some other container. If your reason is "efficiency," measure. Our intuition is most fallible in matters of the performance of container uses.

9.2.1 Elements

Like all standard-library containers, vector is a container of elements of some type T, that is, a vector<T>. Just about any type qualifies as an element type: built-in numeric types (such as char, int, and double), user-defined types (such as string, Entry, list<int>, and Matrix<double,2>), and pointers (such as const char*, Shape*, and double*). When you insert a new element, its value is copied into the container. For example, when you put an integer with the value 7 into a container, the resulting element really has the value 7. The element is not a reference or a pointer to some object containing 7. This makes for nice, compact containers with fast access. For people who care about memory sizes and run-time performance this is critical.

If you have a class hierachy (§4.5) that relies on virtual functions to get polymorphic behavior, do not store objects directly in a container. Instead store a pointer (or a smart pointer; §11.2.1). For example:

```
vector<Shape> vs;                    // No, don't - there is no room for a Circle or a Smiley
vector<Shape*> vps;                  // better, but see §4.5.4
vector<unique_ptr<Shape>> vups;      // OK
```

9.2.2 Range Checking

The standard-library vector does not guarantee range checking. For example:

```
void silly(vector<Entry>& book)
{
    int i = book[book.size()].number;        // book.size() is out of range
    // ...
}
```

That initialization is likely to place some random value in i rather than giving an error. This is undesirable, and out-of-range errors are a common problem. Consequently, I often use a simple range-checking adaptation of vector:

```
template<typename T>
class Vec : public std::vector<T> {
public:
    using vector<T>::vector;                // use the constructors from vector (under the name Vec)

    T& operator[](int i)                    // range check
        { return vector<T>::at(i); }

    const T& operator[](int i) const        // range check const objects; §4.2.1
        { return vector<T>::at(i); }
};
```

`Vec` inherits everything from `vector` except for the subscript operations that it redefines to do range checking. The `at()` operation is a `vector` subscript operation that throws an exception of type `out_of_range` if its argument is out of the `vector`'s range (§3.4.1).

For `Vec`, an out-of-range access will throw an exception that the user can catch. For example:

```
void checked(Vec<Entry>& book)
{
    try {
        book[book.size()] = {"Joe",999999};     // will throw an exception
        // ...
    }
    catch (out_of_range) {
        cout << "range error\n";
    }
}
```

The exception will be thrown, and then caught (§3.4.1). If the user doesn't catch an exception, the program will terminate in a well-defined manner rather than proceeding or failing in an undefined manner. One way to minimize surprises from uncaught exceptions is to use a `main()` with a `try`-block as its body. For example:

```
int main()
try {
    // your code
}
catch (out_of_range) {
    cerr << "range error\n";
}
catch (...) {
    cerr << "unknown exception thrown\n";
}
```

This provides default exception handlers so that if we fail to catch some exception, an error message is printed on the standard error-diagnostic output stream `cerr` (§8.2).

Some implementations save you the bother of defining `Vec` (or equivalent) by providing a range-checked version of `vector` (e.g., as a compiler option).

9.3 list

The standard library offers a doubly-linked list called list:

list:

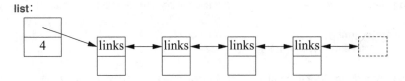

We use a list for sequences where we want to insert and delete elements without moving other elements. Insertion and deletion of phone book entries could be common, so a list could be appropriate for representing a simple phone book. For example:

```
list<Entry> phone_book = {
    {"David Hume",123456},
    {"Karl Popper",234567},
    {"Bertrand Arthur William Russell",345678}
};
```

When we use a linked list, we tend not to access elements using subscripting the way we commonly do for vectors. Instead, we might search the list looking for an element with a given value. To do this, we take advantage of the fact that a list is a sequence as described in Chapter 10:

```
int get_number(const string& s)
{
    for (const auto& x : phone_book)
        if (x.name==s)
            return x.number;
    return 0;   // use 0 to represent "number not found"
}
```

The search for s starts at the beginning of the list and proceeds until s is found or the end of phone_book is reached.

Sometimes, we need to identify an element in a list. For example, we may want to delete it or insert a new entry before it. To do that we use an *iterator*: a list iterator identifies an element of a list and can be used to iterate through a list (hence its name). Every standard-library container provides the functions begin() and end(), which return an iterator to the first and to one-past-the-last element, respectively (Chapter 10). Using iterators explicitly, we can – less elegantly – write the get_number() function like this:

```
int get_number(const string& s)
{
    for (auto p = phone_book.begin(); p!=phone_book.end(); ++p)
        if (p–>name==s)
            return p–>number;
    return 0;   // use 0 to represent "number not found"
}
```

In fact, this is roughly the way the terser and less error-prone range-for loop is implemented by the compiler. Given an iterator **p**, **∗p** is the element to which it refers, **++p** advances **p** to refer to the next element, and when **p** refers to a class with a member **m**, then **p–>m** is equivalent to **(∗p).m**.

Adding elements to a list and removing elements from a list is easy:

```
void f(const Entry& ee, list<Entry>::iterator p, list<Entry>::iterator q)
{
     phone_book.insert(p,ee);       // add ee before the element referred to by p
     phone_book.erase(q);           // remove the element referred to by q
}
```

For a list, **insert(p,elem)** inserts an element with a copy of the value **elem** before the element pointed to by **p**. Here, **p** may be an iterator pointing one-beyond-the-end of the list. Conversely, **erase(p)** removes the element pointed to by **p** and destroys it.

These list examples could be written identically using **vector** and (surprisingly, unless you understand machine architecture) perform better with a small **vector** than with a small list. When all we want is a sequence of elements, we have a choice between using a **vector** and a list. Unless you have a reason not to, use a **vector**. A **vector** performs better for traversal (e.g., **find()** and **count()**) and for sorting and searching (e.g., **sort()** and **binary_search()**).

9.4 map

Writing code to look up a name in a list of *(name,number)* pairs is quite tedious. In addition, a linear search is inefficient for all but the shortest lists. The standard library offers a search tree (a redblack tree) called **map**:

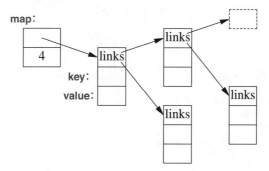

In other contexts, a **map** is known as an associative array or a dictionary. It is implemented as a balanced binary tree.

The standard-library **map** is a container of pairs of values optimized for lookup. We can use the same initializer as for **vector** and list (§9.2, §9.3):

```
map<string,int> phone_book {
     {"David Hume",123456},
     {"Karl Popper",234567},
     {"Bertrand Arthur William Russell",345678}
};
```

When indexed by a value of its first type (called the *key*), a **map** returns the corresponding value of the second type (called the *value* or the *mapped type*). For example:

```
int get_number(const string& s)
{
    return phone_book[s];
}
```

In other words, subscripting a **map** is essentially the lookup we called **get_number()**. If a **key** isn't found, it is entered into the **map** with a default value for its **value**. The default value for an integer type is **0**; the value I just happened to choose represents an invalid telephone number.

If we wanted to avoid entering invalid numbers into our phone book, we could use **find()** and **insert()** instead of [ ].

9.5   unordered_map

The cost of a **map** lookup is **O(log(n))** where **n** is the number of elements in the **map**. That's pretty good. For example, for a **map** with 1,000,000 elements, we perform only about 20 comparisons and indirections to find an element. However, in many cases, we can do better by using a hashed lookup rather than comparison using an ordering function, such as **<**. The standard-library hashed containers are referred to as "unordered" because they don't require an ordering function:

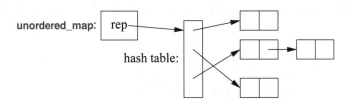

For example, we can use an **unordered_map** from **<unordered_map>** for our phone book:

```
unordered_map<string,int> phone_book {
    {"David Hume",123456},
    {"Karl Popper",234567},
    {"Bertrand Arthur William Russell",345678}
};
```

As for a **map**, we can subscript an **unordered_map**:

```
int get_number(const string& s)
{
    return phone_book[s];
}
```

The standard-library provides a default hash function for **strings** as well as for other built-in and standard-library types. If necessary, you can provide your own. Possibly, the most common need for a "custom" hash function comes when we want an unordered container of one of our own types. A hash function is often provided as a function object (§5.5). For example:

```
struct Record {
    string name;
    int product_code;
    // ...
};

struct Rhash {        // a hash function for Record
    size_t operator()(const Record& r) const
    {
        return hash<string>()(r.name) ^ hash<int>()(r.product_code);
    }
};

unordered_set<Record,Rhash> my_set; // set of Records using Rhash for lookup
```

Creaing a new hash function by combining existing hash functions using exclusive or (ˆ) is simple and often very effective. We often prefer a **set** to a **map** when the key is already part of the data.

9.6 Container Overview

The standard library provides some of the most general and useful container types to allow the programmer to select a container that best serves the needs of an application:

Standard Container Summary	
vector<T>	A variable-size vector (§9.2)
list<T>	A doubly-linked list (§9.3)
forward_list<T>	A singly-linked list
deque<T>	A double-ended queue
set<T>	A set (a **map** with just a key and no value)
multiset<T>	A set in which a value can occur many times
map<K,V>	An associative array (§9.4)
multimap<K,V>	A map in which a key can occur many times
unordered_map<K,V>	A map using a hashed lookup (§9.5)
unordered_multimap<K,V>	A multimap using a hashed lookup
unordered_set<T>	A set using a hashed lookup
unordered_multiset<T>	A multiset using a hashed lookup

The unordered containers are optimized for lookup with a key (often a string); in other words, they are implemented using hash tables.

The containers are defined in namespace **std** and presented in headers <vector>, <list>, <map>, etc. (§6.3). In addition, the standard library provides container adaptors queue<T>, stack<T>, and priority_queue<T>. Look them up if you need them. The standard library also provides more specialized container-like types, such as a fixed-size array array<T,N> (§11.3.1) and bitset<N> (§11.3.2).

The standard containers and their basic operations are designed to be similar from a notational point of view. Furthermore, the meanings of the operations are equivalent for the various containers. Basic operations apply to every kind of container for which they make sense and can be efficiently implemented. For example:

- begin() and end() give iterators to the first and one-beyond-the-last elements, respectively.
- push_back() can be used (efficiently) to add elements to the end of a vector, list, and other containers.
- size() returns the number of elements.

This notational and semantic uniformity enables programmers to provide new container types that can be used in a very similar manner to the standard ones. The range-checked vector, Vector (§3.4.2, Chapter 4), is an example of that. The uniformity of container interfaces allows us to specify algorithms independently of individual container types. However, each has strengths and weaknesses. For example, subscripting and traversing a vector is cheap and easy. On the other hand, vector elements are moved when we insert or remove elements; list has exactly the opposite properties. Please note that a vector is usually more efficient than a list for short sequences of small elements (even for insert() and erase()). I recommend the standard-library vector as the default type for sequences of elements: you need a reason to choose another.

Consider the singly-linked list, forward_list, a container optimized for the empty sequence (which occupies just one word) because the number of elements are zero or very low; such sequences are surprisingly useful.

9.7 Advice

[1] The material in this chapter roughly corresponds to what is described in much greater detail in Chapter 31 of [Stroustrup,2013].
[2] An STL container defines a sequence; §9.2.
[3] STL containers are resource handles; §9.2, §9.3, §9.4, §9.5.
[4] Use vector as your default container; §9.2, §9.6.
[5] For simple traversals of a container, use a range-for loop or a begin/end pair of iterators; §9.2, §9.3.
[6] Use reserve() to avoid invalidating pointers and iterators to elements; §9.2.
[7] Don't assume performance benefits from reserve() without measurement; §9.2.
[8] Use push_back() or resize() on a container rather than realloc() on an array; §9.2.
[9] Don't use iterators into a resized vector; §9.2.
[10] Do not assume that [ ] range checks; §9.2.
[11] Use at() when you need guaranteed range checks; §9.2.
[12] Elements are copied into a container; §9.2.1.
[13] To preserve polymorphic behavior of elements, store pointers; §9.2.1.
[14] Insertion operators, such as insert() and push_back() are often surprisingly efficient on a vector; §9.3.
[15] Use forward_list for sequences that are usually empty; §9.6.
[16] When it comes to performance, don't trust your intuition: measure; §9.2.
[17] A map is usually implemented as a red-black tree; §9.4.
[18] An unordered_map is a hash table; §9.5.

[19]   Pass a container by reference and return a container by value; §9.2.
[20]   For a container, use the ()-initializer syntax for sizes and the {}-initializer syntax for lists of elements; §4.2.3, §9.2.
[21]   Prefer compact and contiguous data structures; §9.3.
[22]   A list is relatively expensive to traverse; §9.3.
[23]   Use unordered containers if you need fast lookup for large amounts of data; §9.5.
[24]   Use ordered associative containers (e.g., map and set) if you need to iterate over their elements in order; §9.4.
[25]   Use unordered containers for element types with no natural order (e.g., no reasonable <); §9.4.
[26]   Experiment to check that you have an acceptable hash function; §9.5.
[27]   Hash function obtained by combining standard hash functions for elements using exclusive or are often good; §9.5.
[28]   Know your standard-library containers and prefer them to hand-crafted data structures; §9.6.

10

Algorithms

Do not multiply entities beyond necessity.
– William Occam

10.1 Introduction

A data structure, such as a list or a vector, is not very useful on its own. To use one, we need operations for basic access such as adding and removing elements (as is provided for **list** and **vector**). Furthermore, we rarely just store objects in a container. We sort them, print them, extract subsets, remove elements, search for objects, etc. Consequently, the standard library provides the most common algorithms for containers in addition to providing the most common container types. For example, we can simply and efficiently sort a **vector** of **Entry**s and place a copy of each unique **vector** element on a **list**:

```
void f(vector<Entry>& vec, list<Entry>& lst)
{
    sort(vec.begin(),vec.end());                    // use < for order
    unique_copy(vec.begin(),vec.end(),lst.begin()); // don't copy adjacent equal elements
}
```

For this to work, less than (**<**) and equal (**==**) must be defined for **Entry**s. For example:

```
bool operator<(const Entry& x, const Entry& y)     // less than
{
    return x.name<y.name;          // order Entrys by their names
}
```

A standard algorithm is expressed in terms of (half-open) sequences of elements. A *sequence* is represented by a pair of iterators specifying the first element and the one-beyond-the-last element:

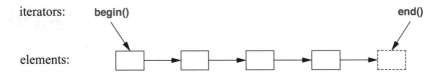

In the example, **sort()** sorts the sequence defined by the pair of iterators **vec.begin()** and **vec.end()** – which just happens to be all the elements of a **vector**. For writing (output), you need only to specify the first element to be written. If more than one element is written, the elements following that initial element will be overwritten. Thus, to avoid errors, **lst** must have at least as many elements as there are unique values in **vec**.

If we wanted to place the unique elements in a new container, we could have written:

```
list<Entry> f(vector<Entry>& vec)
{
    list<Entry> res;
    sort(vec.begin(),vec.end());
    unique_copy(vec.begin(),vec.end(),back_inserter(res));     // append to res
    return res;
}
```

The call **back_inserter(res)** constructs an iterator for **res** that adds elements at the end of a container, extending the container to make room for them. This saves us from first having to allocate a fixed amount of space and then filling it. Thus, the standard containers plus **back_inserter()**s eliminate the need to use error-prone, explicit C-style memory management using **realloc()**. The standard-library **list** has a move constructor (§4.6.2) that makes returning **res** by value efficient (even for **list**s of thousands of elements).

If you find the pair-of-iterators style of code, such as **sort(vec.begin(),vec.end())**, tedious, you can define container versions of the algorithms and write **sort(vec)** (§10.7).

10.2 Use of Iterators

When you first encounter a container, a few iterators referring to useful elements can be obtained; **begin()** and **end()** are the best examples of this. In addition, many algorithms return iterators. For example, the standard algorithm **find** looks for a value in a sequence and returns an iterator to the element found:

```
bool has_c(const string& s, char c)        // does s contain the character c?
{
    auto p = find(s.begin(),s.end(),c);
    if (p!=s.end())
        return true;
    else
        return false;
}
```

Like many standard-library search algorithms, **find** returns **end()** to indicate "not found." An equivalent, shorter, definition of **has_c()** is:

```
bool has_c(const string& s, char c)        // does s contain the character c?
{
    return find(s.begin(),s.end(),c)!=s.end();
}
```

A more interesting exercise would be to find the location of all occurrences of a character in a string. We can return the set of occurrences as a **vector** of **string** iterators. Returning a **vector** is efficient because **vector** provides move semantics (§4.6.1). Assuming that we would like to modify the locations found, we pass a non-**const** string:

```
vector<string::iterator> find_all(string& s, char c)        // find all occurrences of c in s
{
    vector<string::iterator> res;
    for (auto p = s.begin(); p!=s.end(); ++p)
        if (*p==c)
            res.push_back(p);
    return res;
}
```

We iterate through the string using a conventional loop, moving the iterator **p** forward one element at a time using **++** and looking at the elements using the dereference operator *. We could test **find_all()** like this:

```
void test()
{
    string m {"Mary had a little lamb"};
    for (auto p : find_all(m,'a'))
        if (*p!='a')
            cerr << "a bug!\n";
}
```

That call of **find_all()** could be graphically represented like this:

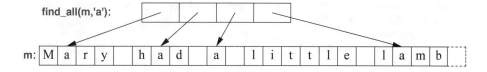

Iterators and standard algorithms work equivalently on every standard container for which their use makes sense. Consequently, we could generalize find_all():

```
template<typename C, typename V>
vector<typename C::iterator> find_all(C& c, V v)          // find all occurrences of v in c
{
     vector<typename C::iterator> res;
     for (auto p = c.begin(); p!=c.end(); ++p)
         if (*p==v)
               res.push_back(p);
     return res;
}
```

The typename is needed to inform the compiler that C's iterator is supposed to be a type and not a value of some type, say, the integer 7. We can hide this implementation detail by introducing a type alias (§5.7) for Iterator:

```
template<typename T>
using Iterator = typename T::iterator;          // T's iterator

template<typename C, typename V>
vector<Iterator<C>> find_all(C& c, V v)          // find all occurrences of v in c
{
     vector<Iterator<C>> res;
     for (auto p = c.begin(); p!=c.end(); ++p)
         if (*p==v)
               res.push_back(p);
     return res;
}
```

We can now write:

```
void test()
{
     string m {"Mary had a little lamb"};

     for (auto p : find_all(m,'a'))          // p is a string::iterator
         if (*p!='a')
               cerr << "string bug!\n";

     list<double> ld {1.1, 2.2, 3.3, 1.1};
     for (auto p : find_all(ld,1.1))
         if (*p!=1.1)
               cerr << "list bug!\n";

     vector<string> vs { "red", "blue", "green", "green", "orange", "green" };
     for (auto p : find_all(vs,"red"))
         if (*p!="red")
               cerr << "vector bug!\n";
```

```
        for (auto p : find_all(vs,"green"))
            *p = "vert";
    }
```

Iterators are used to separate algorithms and containers. An algorithm operates on its data through iterators and knows nothing about the container in which the elements are stored. Conversely, a container knows nothing about the algorithms operating on its elements; all it does is to supply iterators upon request (e.g., **begin()** and **end()**). This model of separation between data storage and algorithm delivers very general and flexible software.

10.3 Iterator Types

What are iterators really? Any particular iterator is an object of some type. There are, however, many different iterator types, because an iterator needs to hold the information necessary for doing its job for a particular container type. These iterator types can be as different as the containers and the specialized needs they serve. For example, a **vector**'s iterator could be an ordinary pointer, because a pointer is quite a reasonable way of referring to an element of a **vector**:

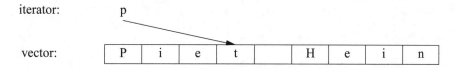

Alternatively, a **vector** iterator could be implemented as a pointer to the **vector** plus an index:

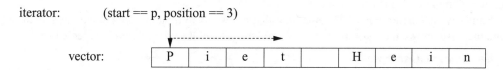

Using such an iterator would allow range checking.

A **list** iterator must be something more complicated than a simple pointer to an element because an element of a **list** in general does not know where the next element of that **list** is. Thus, a **list** iterator might be a pointer to a link:

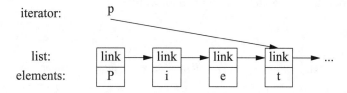

What is common for all iterators is their semantics and the naming of their operations. For example, applying **++** to any iterator yields an iterator that refers to the next element. Similarly, * yields the element to which the iterator refers. In fact, any object that obeys a few simple rules like these is an iterator – *Iterator* is a concept (§5.4). Furthermore, users rarely need to know the type of a specific iterator; each container "knows" its iterator types and makes them available under the conventional names **iterator** and **const_iterator**. For example, **list<Entry>::iterator** is the general iterator type for **list<Entry>**. We rarely have to worry about the details of how that type is defined.

10.4 Stream Iterators

Iterators are a general and useful concept for dealing with sequences of elements in containers. However, containers are not the only place where we find sequences of elements. For example, an input stream produces a sequence of values, and we write a sequence of values to an output stream. Consequently, the notion of iterators can be usefully applied to input and output.

To make an **ostream_iterator**, we need to specify which stream will be used and the type of objects written to it. For example:

```
ostream_iterator<string> oo {cout};        // write strings to cout
```

The effect of assigning to ∗**oo** is to write the assigned value to **cout**. For example:

```
int main()
{
    *oo = "Hello, ";      // meaning cout<<"Hello, "
    ++oo;
    *oo = "world!\n";     // meaning cout<<"world!\n"
}
```

This is yet another way of writing the canonical message to standard output. The **++oo** is done to mimic writing into an array through a pointer.

Similarly, an **istream_iterator** is something that allows us to treat an input stream as a read-only container. Again, we must specify the stream to be used and the type of values expected:

```
istream_iterator<string> ii {cin};
```

Input iterators are used in pairs representing a sequence, so we must provide an **istream_iterator** to indicate the end of input. This is the default **istream_iterator**:

```
istream_iterator<string> eos {};
```

Typically, **istream_iterators** and **ostream_iterators** are not used directly. Instead, they are provided as arguments to algorithms. For example, we can write a simple program to read a file, sort the words read, eliminate duplicates, and write the result to another file:

```
int main()
{
    string from, to;
    cin >> from >> to;                      // get source and target file names

    ifstream is {from};                     // input stream for file "from"
    istream_iterator<string> ii {is};       // input iterator for stream
    istream_iterator<string> eos {};        // input sentinel
```

```
        ofstream os {to};                    // output stream for file "to"
        ostream_iterator<string> oo {os,"\n"};  // output iterator for stream

        vector<string> b {ii,eos};           // b is a vector initialized from input
        sort(b.begin(),b.end());             // sort the buffer

        unique_copy(b.begin(),b.end(),oo);   // copy buffer to output, discard replicated values

        return !is.eof() || !os;             // return error state (§1.3, §8.4)
}
```

An ifstream is an istream that can be attached to a file, and an ofstream is an ostream that can be attached to a file (§8.7). The ostream_iterator's second argument is used to delimit output values.

Actually, this program is longer than it needs to be. We read the strings into a vector, then we sort() them, and then we write them out, eliminating duplicates. A more elegant solution is not to store duplicates at all. This can be done by keeping the strings in a set, which does not keep duplicates and keeps its elements in order (§9.4). That way, we could replace the two lines using a vector with one using a set and replace unique_copy() with the simpler copy():

```
        set<string> b {ii,eos};              // collect strings from input
        copy(b.begin(),b.end(),oo);          // copy buffer to output
```

We used the names ii, eos, and oo only once, so we could further reduce the size of the program:

```
int main()
{
        string from, to;
        cin >> from >> to;                   // get source and target file names

        ifstream is {from};                  // input stream for file "from"
        ofstream os {to};                    // output stream for file "to"

        set<string> b {istream_iterator<string>{is},istream_iterator<string>{}}; // read input
        copy(b.begin(),b.end(),ostream_iterator<string>{os,"\n"});               // copy to output

        return !is.eof() || !os;             // return error state (§1.3, §8.4)
}
```

It is a matter of taste and experience whether or not this last simplification improves readability.

10.5 Predicates

In the examples above, the algorithms have simply "built in" the action to be done for each element of a sequence. However, we often want to make that action a parameter to the algorithm. For example, the find algorithm (§10.2, §10.6) provides a convenient way of looking for a specific value. A more general variant looks for an element that fulfills a specified requirement, a *predicate*. For example, we might want to search a map for the first value larger than 42. A map allows us to access its elements as a sequence of *(key,value)* pairs, so we can search a map<string,int>'s sequence for a pair<const string,int> where the int is greater than 42:

```
void f(map<string,int>& m)
{
    auto p = find_if(m.begin(),m.end(),Greater_than{42});
    // ...
}
```

Here, `Greater_than` is a function object (§5.5) holding the value (42) to be compared against:

```
struct Greater_than {
    int val;
    Greater_than(int v) : val{v} { }
    bool operator()(const pair<string,int>& r) { return r.second>val; }
};
```

Alternatively, we could use a lambda expression (§5.5):

```
auto p = find_if(m.begin(), m.end(), [](const pair<string,int>& r) { return r.second>42; });
```

A predicate should not modify the elements to which it is applied.

10.6 Algorithm Overview

A general definition of an algorithm is "a finite set of rules which gives a sequence of operations for solving a specific set of problems [and] has five important features: Finiteness ... Definiteness ... Input ... Output ... Effectiveness" [Knuth,1968,§1.1]. In the context of the C++ standard library, an algorithm is a function template operating on sequences of elements.

The standard library provides dozens of algorithms. The algorithms are defined in namespace `std` and presented in the `<algorithm>` header. These standard-library algorithms all take sequences as inputs. A half-open sequence from `b` to `e` is referred to as [b:e). Here are a few examples:

Selected Standard Algorithms	
p=find(b,e,x)	p is the first p in [b:e) so that *p==x
p=find_if(b,e,f)	p is the first p in [b:e) so that f(*p)==true
n=count(b,e,x)	n is the number of elements *q in [b:e) so that *q==x
n=count_if(b,e,f)	n is the number of elements *q in [b:e) so that f(*q)
replace(b,e,v,v2)	Replace elements *q in [b:e) so that *q==v by v2
replace_if(b,e,f,v2)	Replace elements *q in [b:e) so that f(*q) by v2
p=copy(b,e,out)	Copy [b:e) to [out:p)
p=copy_if(b,e,out,f)	Copy elements *q from [b:e) so that f(*q) to [out:p)
p=move(b,e,out)	Move [b:e) to [out:p)
p=unique_copy(b,e,out)	Copy [b:e) to [out:p); don't copy adjacent duplicates
sort(b,e)	Sort elements of [b:e) using < as the sorting criterion
sort(b,e,f)	Sort elements of [b:e) using f as the sorting criterion
(p1,p2)=equal_range(b,e,v)	[p1:p2) is the subsequence of the sorted sequence [b:e) with the value v; basically a binary search for v
p=merge(b,e,b2,e2,out)	Merge two sorted sequences [b:e) and [b2:e2) into [out:p)

These algorithms, and many more (e.g., §12.3), can be applied to elements of containers, strings, and built-in arrays.

Some algorithms, such as replace() and sort(), modify element values, but no algorithm add or subtract elements of a container. The reason is that a sequence does not identify the container that holds the elements of the sequence. If you want to add elements, you need something, such as a back_inserter that knows about the container (§10.1), or directly refer to the container itself, such as push_back() or erase() (§9.2).

The standard-library algorithms tend to be more carefully designed, specified, and implemented than the average hand-crafted loop, so know them and use them in preference to code written in the bare language.

10.7 Container Algorithms

A sequence is defined by a pair of iterators [begin:end). This is general and flexible, but most often, we apply an algorithm to a sequence that is the contents of a container. For example:

```
sort(v.begin(),v.end());
```

Why don't we just say sort(v)? We can easily provide that shorthand:

```
namespace Estd {
    using namespace std;

    template<typename C>
    void sort(C& c)
    {
        sort(c.begin(),c.end());
    }

    template<typename C, typename Pred>
    void sort(C& c, Pred p)
    {
        sort(c.begin(),c.end(),p);
    }

    // ...
}
```

I put the container versions of sort() (and other algorithms) into their own namespace Estd ("extended std") to avoid interfering with other programmers' uses of namespace std.

10.8 Advice

[1]   The material in this chapter roughly corresponds to what is described in much greater detail in Chapter 32 of [Stroustrup,2013].

[2]   An STL algorithm operates on one or more sequences; §10.1.

[3]   An input sequence is half-open and defined by a pair of iterators; §10.1.

[4]   When searching, an algorithm usually returns the end of the input sequence to indicate "not found"; §10.2.

[5]   Algorithms do not directly add or subtract elements from their argument sequences; §10.2, §10.6.

[6]   When writing a loop, consider whether it could be expressed as a general algorithm; §10.2.

[7]   Use predicates and other function objects to give standard algorithms a wider range of meanings; §10.5, §10.6.

[8]   A predicate must not modify its argument; §10.5.

[9]   Know your standard-library algorithms and prefer them to hand-crafted loops; §10.6.

[10]   When the pair-of-iterators style becomes tedious, introduce a container/range algorithm; §10.7.

11

Utilities

The time you enjoy wasting is not wasted time.
– Bertrand Russell

- Introduction
- Resource Management
  unique_ptr and **shared_ptr**
- Specialized Containers
  array; **bitset**; **pair** and **tuple**
- Time
- Function Adaptors
  bind(); **mem_fn()**; **function**
- Type Functions
  iterator_traits; Type Predicates
- Advice

11.1 Introduction

Not all standard-library components come as part of obviously labeled facilities, such as "containers" or "I/O." This section gives a few examples of small, widely useful components. The point here is that a function or a type need not be complicated or closely tied to a mass of other functions and types to be useful. Such library components mostly act as building blocks for more powerful library facilities, including other components of the standard library.

11.2 Resource Management

One of the key tasks of any nontrivial program is to manage resources. A resource is something that must be acquired and later (explicitly or implicitly) released. Examples are memory, locks, sockets, thread handles, and file handles. For a long-running program, failing to release a resource in a timely manner ("a leak") can cause serious performance degradation and possibly even a miserable crash. Even for short programs, a leak can become an embarrassment, say by a resource shortage increasing the run time by orders of magnitude.

The standard library components are designed not to leak resources. To do this, they rely on the basic language support for resource management using constructor/destructor pairs to ensure that a resource doesn't outlive an object responsible for it. The use of a constructor/destructor pair in **Vector** to manage the lifetime of its elements is an example (§4.2.2) and all standard-library containers are implemented in similar ways. Importantly, this approach interacts correctly with error handling using exceptions. For example, the technique is used for the standard-library lock classes:

```
mutex m;  // used to protect access to shared data
// ...
void f()
{
    unique_lock<mutex> lck {m};  // acquire the mutex m
    // ... manipulate shared data ...
}
```

A **thread** will not proceed until **lck**'s constructor has acquired its **mutex**, m (§13.5). The corresponding destructor releases the resource. So, in this example, **unique_lock**'s destructor releases the **mutex** when the thread of control leaves f() (through a **return**, by "falling off the end of the function," or through an exception throw).

This is an application of the "Resource Acquisition Is Initialization" technique (RAII; §4.2.2). RAII is fundamental to the idiomatic handling of resources in C++. Containers (such as **vector** and **map**), **string**, and **iostream** manage their resources (such as file handles and buffers) similarly.

11.2.1 unique_ptr and shared_ptr

The examples so far take care of objects defined in a scope, releasing the resources they acquire at the exit from the scope, but what about objects allocated on the free store? In **<memory>**, the standard library provides two "smart pointers" to help manage objects on the free store:
[1]   **unique_ptr** to represent unique ownership
[2]   **shared_ptr** to represent shared ownership
The most basic use of these "smart pointers" is to prevent memory leaks caused by careless programming. For example:

```
void f(int i, int j)      // X* vs. unique_ptr<X>
{
    X* p = new X;                    // allocate a new X
    unique_ptr<X> sp {new X};        // allocate a new X and give its pointer to unique_ptr
    // ...
    if (i<99) throw Z{};             // may throw an exception
    if (j<77) return;                // may return "early"
    // ...
    p->do_something();               // may throw an exception
    sp->do_something();              // may throw an exception
```

```
    // ...
    delete p;                        // destroy *p
}
```

Here, we "forgot" to delete p if i<99 or if j<77. On the other hand, unique_ptr ensures that its object is properly destroyed whichever way we exit f() (by throwing an exception, by executing return, or by "falling off the end"). Ironically, we could have solved the problem simply by *not* using a pointer and *not* using new:

```
void f(int i, int j)      // use a local variable
{
    X x;
    // ...
}
```

Unfortunately, overuse of new (and of pointers and references) seems to be an increasing problem.

However, when you really need the semantics of pointers, unique_ptr is a very lightweight mechanism with no space or time overhead compared to correct use of a built-in pointer. Its further uses include passing free-store allocated objects in and out of functions:

```
unique_ptr<X> make_X(int i)
    // make an X and immediately give it to a unique_ptr
{
    // ... check i, etc. ...
    return unique_ptr<X>{new X{i}};
}
```

A unique_ptr is a handle to an individual object (or an array) in much the same way that a vector is a handle to a sequence of objects. Both control the lifetime of other objects (using RAII) and both rely on move semantics to make return simple and efficient.

The shared_ptr is similar to unique_ptr except that shared_ptrs are copied rather than moved. The shared_ptrs for an object share ownership of an object and that object is destroyed when the last of its shared_ptrs is destroyed. For example:

```
void f(shared_ptr<fstream>);
void g(shared_ptr<fstream>);

void user(const string& name, ios_base::openmode mode)
{
    shared_ptr<fstream> fp {new fstream(name,mode)};
    if (!*fp)                        // make sure the file was properly opened
        throw No_file{};

    f(fp);
    g(fp);
    // ...
}
```

Now, the file opened by fp's constructor will be closed by the last function to (explicitly or implicitly) destroy a copy of fp. Note that f() or g() may spawn a task holding a copy of fp or in some other way store a copy that outlives user(). Thus, shared_ptr provides a form of garbage collection that respects the destructor-based resource management of the memory-managed objects. This is neither cost free nor exorbitantly expensive, but it does make the lifetime of the shared object hard to predict. Use shared_ptr only if you actually need shared ownership.

Creating an object on the free store and then passing a pointer to it to a smart pointer is logically a bit odd and can be verbose. To compensate, the standard library (in <memory>) provides a function make_shared(). For example:

```
struct S {
    int i;
    string s;
    double d;
    // ...
};

shared_ptr<S> p1 {new S {1,"Ankh Morpork",4.65}};

auto p2 = make_shared<S>(2,"Oz",7.62);
```

Now, p2 is a shared_ptr<S> pointing to an object of type S allocated on the free store, containing {2,string{"Oz",7.62}.

Currently, there is no standard-library make_unique() similar to make_shared() and make_pair() (§11.3.3). However, it is easily defined:

```
template<typename T, typename... Args>
unique_ptr<T> make_unique(Args&&... args)
{
    return std::unique_ptr<T>{new T{std::forward<Args>(args)...}};
}
```

No, I don't claim that this definition is trivial to understand, but it is efficient and quite general. The elipses, ..., indicate the use of a variadic template (§5.6). We use std::forward() to forward arguments without overhead or loss of information. We can now write:

```
auto p2 = make_unique<S>(3,"Atlantis",11.3);
```

Given unique_ptr and shared_ptr, we can implement a complete "no naked new" policy (§4.2.2) for many programs. However, these "smart pointers" are still conceptually pointers and therefore only my second choice for resource management – after containers and other types that manage their resources at a higher conceptual level. In particular, shared_ptrs do not in themselves provide any rules for which of their owners can read and/or write the shared object. Data races (§13.7) and other forms of confusion are not addressed simply by eliminating the resource management issues.

Where do we use "smart pointers" (such as unique_ptr) rather than resource handles with operations designed specifically for the resource (such as vector or thread)? Unsurprisingly, the answer is "when we need pointer semantics."

- When we share an object, we need pointers (or references) to refer to the shared object, so a shared_ptr becomes the obvious choice (unless there is an obvious single owner).
- When we refer to a polymorphic object, we need a pointer (or a reference) because we don't know the exact type of the object referred to (or even its size), so a unique_ptr becomes the obvious choice.

  • A shared polymorphic object typically requires shared_ptrs.
We do *not* need to use a pointer to return a collection of objects from a function; a container that is
a resource handle will do that simply and efficiently (§4.6.2).

11.3 Specialized Containers

The standard library provides several containers that don't fit perfectly into the STL framework
(Chapter 9, Chapter 10). Examples are built-in arrays, array, and string. I sometimes refer to those
as "almost containers," but that is not quite fair: they hold elements, so they are containers, but
each has restrictions or added facilities that make them awkward in the context of the STL.
Describing them separately also simplifies the description of the STL.

"Almost Containers"	
T[N]	Built-in array: a fixed-size continuously allocated sequence of N elements of type T; implicitly converts to a T*
array<T,N>	A fixed-size continuously allocated sequence of N elements of type T; like the built-in array, but with most problems solved
bitset<N>	A fixed-size sequence of N bits
vector<bool>	A sequence of bits compactly stored in a specialization of vector
pair<T,U>	Two elements of types T and U
tuple<T...>	A sequence of an arbitrary number of elements of arbitrary types
basic_string<C>	A sequence of characters of type C; provides string operations
valarray<T>	An array of numeric values of type T; provides numeric operations

Why does the standard library provide so many containers? They serve common but different
(often overlapping) needs. If the standard library didn't provide them, many people would have to
design and implement their own. For example:
  • pair and tuple are heterogeneous; all other containers are homogeneous (all elements are of
     the same type).
  • array, vector, and tuple elements are contiguously allocated; forward_list and map are linked
     structures.
  • bitset and vector<bool> hold bits and access them through proxy objects; all other standard-
     library containers can hold a variety of types and access elements directly.
  • basic_string requires its elements to be some form of character and to provide string manip-
     ulation, such as concatenation and locale-sensitive operations
  • valarray requires its elements to be numbers and to provide numerical operations.
All of these containers can be seen as providing specialized services needed by large communities
of programmers. No single container could serve all of these needs because some needs are contra-
dictory, for example, "ability to grow" vs. "guaranteed to be allocated in a fixed location," and
"elements do not move when elements are added" vs. "contiguously allocated." Furthermore, a
very general container would imply overhead deemed unacceptable for individual containers.

11.3.1 array

An **array**, defined in **<array>**, is a fixed-size sequence of elements of a given type where the number of elements is specified at compile time. Thus, an **array** can be allocated with its elements on the stack, in an object, or in static storage. The elements are allocated in the scope where the **array** is defined. An **array** is best understood as a built-in array with its size firmly attached, without implicit, potentially surprising conversions to pointer types, and with a few convenience functions provided. There is no overhead (time or space) involved in using an **array** compared to using a built-in array. An **array** does *not* follow the "handle to elements" model of STL containers. Instead, an **array** directly contains its elements.

An **array** can be initialized by an initializer list:

```
array<int,3> a1 = {1,2,3};
```

The number of elements in the initializer must be equal to or less than the number of elements specified for the **array**.

The element count is not optional:

```
array<int> ax = {1,2,3};        // error size not specified
```

The element count must be a constant expression:

```
void f(int n)
{
    array<string,n> aa = {"John's", "Queens' "};    // error: size not a constant expression
    //
}
```

If you need the element count to be a variable, use **vector**.

When necessary, an **array** can be explicitly passed to a C-style function that expects a pointer. For example:

```
void f(int* p, int sz);      // C-style interface

void g()
{
    array<int,10> a;

    f(a,a.size());              // error: no conversion
    f(&a[0],a.size());          // C-style use
    f(a.data(),a.size());       // C-style use

    auto p = find(a.begin(),a.end(),777);     // C++/STL-style use
    // ...
}
```

Why would we use an **array** when **vector** is so much more flexible? Because an **array** is less flexible, it is simpler. Occasionally, there is a significant performance advantage to be had by directly accessing elements allocated on the stack rather than allocating elements on the free store, accessing them indirectly through the **vector** (a handle), and then deallocating them. On the other hand, the stack is a limited resource (especially on some embedded systems), and stack overflow is nasty.

Why would we use an **array** when we could use a built-in array? An **array** knows its size, so it is easy to use with standard-library algorithms, and it can be copied (using = or initialization). However, my main reason to prefer **array** is that it saves me from surprising nasty conversions to pointers. Consider:

```
void h()
{
    Circle a1[10];
    array<Circle,10> a2;
    // ...
    Shape* p1 = a1;      // OK: disaster waiting to happen
    Shape* p2 = a2;      // error: no conversion of array<Circle,10> to Shape*
    p1[3].draw();        // disaster
}
```

The "disaster" comment assumes that **sizeof(Shape)<sizeof(Circle)**, so that subscripting a **Circle[]** through a **Shape*** gives a wrong offset. All standard containers provide this advantage over built-in arrays.

11.3.2 bitset

Aspects of a system, such as the state of an input stream, are often represented as a set of flags indicating binary conditions such as good/bad, true/false, and on/off. C++ supports the notion of small sets of flags efficiently through bitwise operations on integers (§1.5). Class **bitset<N>** generalizes this notion and offers greater convenience by providing operations on a sequence of N bits [0:N), where N is known at compile time. For sets of bits that don't fit into a **long long int**, using a **bitset** is much more convenient than using integers directly. For smaller sets, **bitset** is usually optimized. If you want to name the bits, rather than numbering them, you can use a **set** (§9.4) or an enumeration (§2.5).

A **bitset** can be initialized with an integer or a string:

```
bitset<9> bs1 {"110001111"};
bitset<9> bs2 {399};
```

The usual bitwise operations (§1.5) can be applied, as can left- and right-shift operations (<< and >>):

```
bitset<9> bs3 = ~bs1;        // complement: bs3=="001110000"
bitset<9> bs4 = bs1&bs3;     // all zeros
bitset<9> bs5 = bs1<<2;      // shift left: bs5 = "000111100"
```

The shift operators (here, <<) "shifts in" zeros.

The operations **to_ullong()** and **to_string()** provide the inverse operations to the constructors. For example, we could write out the binary representation of an **int**:

```
void binary(int i)
{
    bitset<8*sizeof(int)> b = i;      // assume 8-bit byte (see also §12.7)
    cout << b.to_string() << '\n';    // write out the bits of i
}
```

This prints the bits represented as 1s and 0s from left to right, with the most significant bit leftmost, so that argument 123 would give the output

```
00000000000000000000000001111011
```

For this example, it is simpler to directly use the bitset output operator:

```
void binary2(int i)
{
    bitset<8*sizeof(int)> b = i;      // assume 8-bit byte (see also §12.7)
    cout << b << '\n';                // write out the bits of i
}
```

11.3.3 pair and tuple

Often, we need some data that is just data; that is, a collection of values, rather than an object of a class with a well-defined semantics and an invariant for its value (§3.4.2). In such cases, we could define a simple struct with an appropriate set of appropriately named members. Alternatively, we could let the standard library write the definition for us. For example, the standard-library algorithm equal_range returns a pair of iterators specifying a subsequence meeting a predicate:

```
template<typename Forward_iterator, typename T, typename Compare>
    pair<Forward_iterator,Forward_iterator>
    equal_range(Forward_iterator first, Forward_iterator last, const T& val, Compare cmp);
```

Given a sorted sequence [first:last), equal_range() will return the pair representing the subsequence that matches the predicate cmp. We can use that to search in a sorted sequence of Records:

```
auto rec_lt = [](const Record& r1, const Record& r2) { return r1.name<r2.name;};      // compare names

void f(const vector<Record>& v)          // assume that v is sorted on its "name" field
{
    auto er = equal_range(v.begin(),v.end(),Record{"Reg"},rec_lt);

    for (auto p = er.first; p!=er.second; ++p)      // print all equal records
        cout << *p;                                 // assume that << is defined for Record
}
```

The first member of a pair is called first and the second member is called second. This naming is not particularly creative and may look a bit odd at first, but such consistent naming is a boon when we want to write generic code.

The standard-library pair (from <utility>) is quite frequently used in the standard library and elsewhere. A pair provides operators, such as =, ==, and <, if its elements do. The make_pair() function makes it easy to create a pair without explicitly mentioning its type. For example:

```
void f(vector<string>& v)
{
    auto pp = make_pair(v.begin(),2);    // pp is a pair<vector<string>::iterator,int>
    // ...
}
```

If you need more than two elements (or less), you can use **tuple** (from **<utility>**). A **tuple** is a heterogeneous sequence of elements; for example:

```
tuple<string,int,double> t2 {"Sild",123,3.14};        // the type is explicitly specified

auto t = make_tuple(string{"Herring"},10,1.23);       // the type is deduced to tuple<string,int,double>

string s = get<0>(t);       // get first element of tuple: "Herring"
int x = get<1>(t);          // 10
double d = get<2>(t);       // 1.23
```

The elements of a **tuple** are numbered (starting with zero), rather than named the way elements of
pairs are (**first** and **second**). To get compile-time selection of elements, I must unfortunately use the
ugly **get<1>(t)**, rather than **get(t,1)** or **t[1]**.

Like **pairs**, **tuples** can be assigned and compared if their elements can be.

A **pair** is common in interfaces because often we want to return more than one value, such as a
result and an indicator of the quality of that result. It is less common to need three or more parts to
a result, so **tuples** are more often found in the implementations of generic algorithms.

11.4 Time

The standard library provides facilities for dealing with time. For example, here is the basic way of
timing something:

```
using namespace std::chrono;      // see §3.3

auto t0 = high_resolution_clock::now();
do_work();
auto t1 = high_resolution_clock::now();
cout << duration_cast<milliseconds>(t1−t0).count() << "msec\n";
```

The clock returns a **time_point** (a point in time). Subtracting two **time_points** gives a **duration** (a
period of time). Various clocks give their results in various units of time (the clock I used measures
nanoseconds), so it is usually a good idea to convert a **duration** into a known unit. That's what **dura-
tion_cast** does.

The standard-library facilities for dealing with time are found in the subnamespace **std::chrono**
in **<chrono>**.

Don't make statements about "efficiency" of code without first doing time measurements.
Guesses about performance are most unreliable.

11.5 Function Adaptors

A function adaptor takes a function as argument and returns a function object that can be used to
invoke the original function. The standard library provides **bind()** and **mem_fn()** adaptors to do argument binding, also called *Currying* or *partial evaluation*. Binders were heavily used in the past, but
most uses seem to be more easily expressed using lambdas (§5.5).

11.5.1 bind()

Given a function and a set of arguments, bind() produces a function object that can be called with "the remaining" arguments, if any, of the function. For example:

```
double cube(double);

auto cube2 = bind(cube,2);
```

A call cube2() will invoke cube with the argument 2, that is, cube(2). We don't have to bind every argument of a function. For example:

```
using namespace placeholders;

void f(int,const string&);
auto g = bind(f,2,_1);        // bind f()'s first argument to 2
f(2,"hello");
g("hello");                   // also calls f(2,"hello");
```

The curious _1 argument to the binder is a placeholder telling bind() where arguments to the resulting function object should go. In this case, g()'s (first) argument is used as f()'s second argument.

The placeholders are found in the (sub)namespace std::placeholders that is part of <functional>.

To bind arguments for an overloaded function, we have to explicitly state which version of the function we want to bind:

```
int pow(int,int);
double pow(double,double);   // pow() is overloaded

auto pow2 = bind(pow,_1,2);                              // error: which pow()?
auto pow2 = bind((double(*)(double,double))pow,_1,2);   // OK (but ugly)
```

I assigned the result of bind() to a variable declared using auto. This saves me the bother of specifying the return type of a call of bind(). That can be useful because the return type of bind() is unspecified because it varies with the type of function to be called and the argument values stored. In particular, the returned function object is larger when it has to hold values of bound parameters. When we want to be specific about the types of the arguments required and the type of result returned, we can use a function (§11.5.3).

11.5.2 mem_fn()

The function adaptor mem_fn(mf) produces a function object that can be called as a nonmember function. For example:

```
void user(Shape* p)
{
    p->draw();
    auto draw = mem_fn(&Shape::draw);
    draw(p);
}
```

The major use of mem_fn() is when an algorithm requires an operation to be called as a nonmember function. For example:

```
void draw_all(vector<Shape*>& v)
{
    for_each(v.begin(),v.end(),mem_fn(&Shape::draw));
}
```

Thus, mem_fn() can be seen as a mapping from the object-oriented calling style to the functional one.

Often, lambdas provide a simple and general alternative to binders. For example:

```
void draw_all(vector<Shape*>& v)
{
    for_each(v.begin(),v.end(),[](Shape* p) { p–>draw(); });
}
```

11.5.3 function

A bind() can be used directly, and it can be used to initialize an auto variable. In that, bind() resembles a lambda.

If we want to assign the result of bind() to a variable with a specific type, we can use the standard-library type function. A function is specified with a specific return type and a specific argument type. For example:

```
int f1(double);
function<int(double)> fct {f1}; // initialize to f1
int f2(string);

void user()
{
    fct = [](double d) { return round(d); };   // assign lambda to fct
    fct = f1;                                    // assign function to fct
    fct = f2;                                    // error: incorrect argument type
                                                 // (f2 cannot be called with a double argument)
}
```

The standard-library function is a type that can hold any object you can invoke using the call operator (). That is, an object of type function is a function object (§5.5). For example:

```
int round(double x) { return static_cast<int>(floor(x+0.5)); }  // conventional 4/5 rounding (from <cmath>)

function<int(double)> f;  // f can hold anything that can be called with a double and return an int

enum class Round_style { truncate, round };

struct Round {          // function object carrying a state
    Round_style s;
    Round(Round_style ss) :s(ss) { }
    int operator()(double x) const { return static_cast<int>((s==Round_style::round) ? (x+0.5) : x); }
};
```

I use static_cast (§14.2.3) to make it explicit that I want to return an int.

```
void t1()
{
    f = round;
    cout << f(7.6) << '\n';                          // call through f to the function

    f = Round(Round_style::truncate);
    cout << f(7.6) << '\n';                          // call through f to the function object

    Round_style style = Round_style::round;
    f = [style] (double x){ return static_cast<int>((style==Round_style::round) ? x+0.5 : x); };

    cout << f(7.6) << '\n';                          // call through f to the lambda

    vector<double> v {7.6};
    f = Round(Round_style::round);
    std::transform(v.begin(),v.end(),v.begin(),f);   // pass f to the transform() algorithm

    cout << v[0] << '\n';                            // transformed by the function object
}
```

We get 8, 7, 8, and 8.

Obviously, **functions** are useful for callbacks, for passing operations as arguments, etc.

11.6   Type Functions

A *type function* is a function that is evaluated at compile-time given a type as its argument or returning a type. The standard library provides a variety of type functions to help library implementers and programmers in general to write code that take advantage of aspects of the language, the standard library, and code in general.

For numerical types, **numeric_limits** from **<limits>** presents a variety of useful information (§12.7). For example:

```
constexpr float min = numeric_limits<float>::min();      // smallest positive float
```

Similarly, object sizes can be found by the built-in **sizeof** operator (§1.5). For example:

```
constexpr int szi = sizeof(int);      // the number of bytes in an int
```

Such type functions are part of C++'s mechanisms for compile-time computation that allow tighter type checking and better performance than would otherwise have been possible. Use of such features is often called *metaprogramming* or (when templates are involved) *template metaprogramming*. Here, I just present two facilities provided by the standard library: **iterator_traits** (§11.6.1) and type predicates (§11.6.2).

11.6.1 iterator_traits

The standard-library **sort()** takes a pair of iterators supposed to define a sequence (Chapter 10). Furthermore, those iterators must offer random access to that sequence, that is, they must be *random-access iterators*. Some containers, such as forward_list, do not offer that. In particular, a forward_list is a singly-linked list so subscripting would be expensive and there is no reasonable way to refer back to a previous element. However, like most containers, forward_list offers *forward iterators* that can be used to traverse the sequence by algorithms and for-statements (§5.2).

The standard library provides a mechanism, iterator_traits that allows us to check which kind of iterator is provided. Given that, we can improve the range sort() from §10.7 to accept either a vector or a forward_list. For example:

```
void test(vector<string>& v, forward_list<int>& lst)
{
    sort(v);   // sort the vector
    sort(lst); // sort the singly-linked list
}
```

The techniques needed to make that work are generally useful.

First, I write two helper functions that take an extra argument indicating whether they are to be used for random-access iterators or forward iterators. The version taking random-access iterator arguments is trivial:

```
template<typename Ran>                                      // for random-access iterators
void sort_helper(Ran beg, Ran end, random_access_iterator_tag)   // we can subscript into [beg:end)
{
    sort(beg,end);      // just sort it
}
```

The version for forward iterators simply copies the list into a vector, sorts, and copies back:

```
template<typename For>                                      // for forward iterators
void sort_helper(For beg, For end, forward_iterator_tag)    // we can traverse [beg:end)
{
    vector<Value_type<For>> v {beg,end};   // initialize a vector from [beg:end)
    sort(v.begin(),v.end());
    copy(v.begin(),v.end(),beg);           // copy the elements back
}
```

Value_type<For>> is the type of For's elements, called it's *value type*. Every standard-library iterator has a member value_type. I get the Value_type<For>> notation by defining a type alias (§5.7):

```
template<typename C>
    using Value_type = typename C::value_type; // C's value type
```

Thus, v is a vector<X> where X is the element type of the input sequence.

The real "type magic" is in the selection of helper functions:

```
template<typename C>
void sort(C& c)
{
    using Iter = Iterator_type<C>;
    sort_helper(c.begin(),c.end(),Iterator_category<Iter>{});
}
```

Here, I use two type functions: Iterator_type<C> returns the iterator type of C (that is, C::iterator) and then Iterator_category<Iter>{} constructs a "tag" value indicating the kind of iterator provided:

- std::random_access_iterator_tag if C's iterator supports random access.
- std::forward_iterator_tag if C's iterator supports forward iteration.

Given that, we can select between the two sorting algorithms at compile time. This technique, called *tag dispatch* is one of several used in the standard library and elsewhere to improve flexibility and performance.

The standard-library support for techniques for using iterators, such as tag dispatch, comes in the form of a simple class template iterator_traits from <iterator>. This allows simple definitions of the type functions used in sort():

```
template<typename C>
    using Iterator_type = typename C::iterator;    // C's iterator type
```

```
template<typename Iter>
    using Iterator_category = typename std::iterator_traits<Iter>::iterator_category;   // Iter's category
```

If you don't want to know what kind of "compile-time type magic" is used to provide the standard-library features, you are free to ignore facilities such as iterator_traits. But then you can't use the techniques they support to improve your own code.

11.6.2 Type Predicates

A standard-library type predicate is a simple type function that answers a fundamental question about types. For example:

```
bool b1 = Is_arithmetic<int>();     // yes, int is an arithmetic type
bool b2 = Is_arithmetic<string>();  // no, std::string is not an arithmetic type
```

These predicates are found in <type_traits>. Other examples are is_class, is_pod, is_literal_type, has_virtual_destructor, and is_base_of. They are most useful when we write templates. For example:

```
template<typename Scalar>
class complex {
    Scalar re, im;
public:
    static_assert(Is_arithmetic<Scalar>(), "Sorry, I only support complex of arithmetic types");
    // ...
};
```

To improve readability compared to using the standard library directly, I defined a type function:

```
template<typename T>
constexpr bool Is_arithmetic()
{
    return std::is_arithmetic<T>::value ;
}
```

Older programs use ::value directly instead of (), but I consider that quite ugly and it exposes implementation details.

11.7 Advice

[1] The material in this chapter roughly corresponds to what is described in much greater detail in Chapters 33-35 of [Stroustrup,2013].

[2] A library doesn't have to be large or complicated to be useful; §11.1.

[3] A resource is anything that has to be acquired and (explicitly or implicitly) released; §11.2.

[4] Use resource handles to manage resources (RAII); §11.2.

[5] Use **unique_ptr** to refer to objects of polymorphic type; §11.2.1.

[6] Use **shared_ptr** to refer to shared objects; §11.2.1.

[7] Prefer resource handles with specific semantics to smart pointers; §11.2.1.

[8] Prefer **unique_ptr** to **shared_ptr**; §4.6.4, §11.2.1.

[9] Prefer smart pointers to garbage collection; §4.6.4, §11.2.1.

[10] Use **array** where you need a sequence with a **constexpr** size; §11.3.1.

[11] Prefer **array** over built-in arrays; §11.3.1.

[12] Use **bitset** if you need **N** bits and **N** is not necessarily the number of bits in a built-in integer type; §11.3.2.

[13] When using **pair**, consider **make_pair()** for type deduction; §11.3.3.

[14] When using **tuple**, consider **make_tuple()** for type deduction; §11.3.3.

[15] Time your programs before making claims about efficiency; §11.4.

[16] Use **duration_cast** to report time measurements with proper units; §11.4.

[17] Often, a lambda is an alternative to using **bind()** or **mem_fn()**; §11.5.

[18] Use **bind()** to create variants of functions and function objects; §11.5.1.

[19] Use **mem_fn()** to create function objects that can invoke a member function when called using the traditional function call notation; §11.5.2.

[20] Use **function** when you need to store something that can be called; §11.5.3.

[21] You can write code to explicitly depend on properties of types; §11.6.

12

Numerics

The purpose of computing is insight, not numbers.
– R. W. Hamming

... but for the student,
numbers are often the best road to insight.
– A. Ralston

- Introduction
- Mathematical Functions
- Numerical Algorithms
- Complex Numbers
- Random Numbers
- Vector Arithmetic
- Numeric Limits
- Advice

12.1 Introduction

C++ was not designed primarily with numeric computation in mind. However, numeric computation typically occurs in the context of other work – such as database access, networking, instrument control, graphics, simulation, and financial analysis – so C++ becomes an attractive vehicle for computations that are part of a larger system. Furthermore, numeric methods have come a long way from being simple loops over vectors of floating-point numbers. Where more complex data structures are needed as part of a computation, C++'s strengths become relevant. The net effect is that C++ is widely used for scientific, engineering, financial, and other computation involving sophisticated numerics. Consequently, facilities and techniques supporting such computation have emerged. This chapter describes the parts of the standard library that support numerics.

12.2 Mathematical Functions

In <cmath>, we find the *standard mathematical functions*, such as sqrt(), log(), and sin() for arguments of type float, double, and long double:

Standard Mathematical Functions	
abs(x)	Absolute value
ceil(x)	Smallest integer >= x
floor(x)	Largest integer <= x
sqrt(x)	Square root; x must be non-negative
cos(x)	Cosine
sin(x)	Sine
tan(x)	Tangent
acos(x)	Arccosine; the result is non-negative
asin(x)	Arcsine; the result nearest to 0 is returned
atan(x)	Arctangent
sinh(x)	Hyperbolic sine
cosh(x)	Hyperbolic cosine
tanh(x)	Hyperbolic tangent
exp(x)	Base e exponential
log(x)	Natural logarithm, base e; x must be positive
log10(x)	Base 10 logarithm

The versions for complex (§12.4) are found in <complex>. For each function, the return type is the same as the argument type.

Errors are reported by setting errno from <cerrno> to EDOM for a domain error and to ERANGE for a range error. For example:

```
void f()
{
    errno = 0; // clear old error state
    sqrt(-1);
    if (errno==EDOM)
        cerr << "sqrt() not defined for negative argument";

    errno = 0; // clear old error state
    pow(numeric_limits<double>::max(),2);
    if (errno == ERANGE)
        cerr << "result of pow() too large to represent as a double";
}
```

A few more mathematical functions are found in <cstdlib> and there is a separate ISO standard for *special mathematical functions* [C++Math,2010].

12.3 Numerical Algorithms

In <numeric>, we find a small set of generalized numerical algorithms, such as accumulate().

Numerical Algorithms (§iso.26.7)	
x=accumulate(b,e,i)	x is the sum of i and the elements of [b:e)
x=accumulate(b,e,i,f)	accumulate using f instead of +
x=inner_product(b,e,b2,i)	x is the inner product of [b:e) and [b2:b2+(e–b)), that is, the sum of i and (*p1)*(*p2) for each p1 in [b:e) and the corresponding p2 in [b2:b2+(e–b))
x=inner_product(b,e,b2,i,f,f2)	inner_product using f and f2 instead of + and *
p=partial_sum(b,e,out)	Element i of [out:p) is the sum of elements [b:b+i]
p=partial_sum(b,e,out,f)	partial_sum using f instead of +
p=adjacent_difference(b,e,out)	Element i of [out:p) is (*b+i)–*(b+i–1) for i>0; if e–b>0, then *out is *b
p=adjacent_difference(b,e,out,f)	adjacent_difference using f instead of –
iota(b,e,v)	For each element in [b:e) assign ++v; thus the sequence becomes v+1, v+2, ...

These algorithms generalize common operations such as computing a sum by letting them apply to all kinds of sequences and by making the operation applied to elements of those sequences a parameter. For each algorithm, the general version is supplemented by a version applying the most common operator for that algorithm. For example:

```
void f()
{
      list<double> lst {1, 2, 3, 4, 5, 9999.99999};
      auto s = accumulate(lst.begin(),lst.end(),0.0); // calculate the sum
      cout << s << '\n';                    // print 10014.9999
}
```

These algorithms work for every standard-library sequence and can have operations supplied as arguments (§12.3).

12.4 Complex Numbers

The standard library supports a family of complex number types along the lines of the complex class described in §4.2.1. To support complex numbers where the scalars are single-precision floating-point numbers (floats), double-precision floating-point numbers (doubles), etc., the standard library complex is a template:

```
template<typename Scalar>
class complex {
public:
      complex(const Scalar& re ={}, const Scalar& im ={});
      // ...
};
```

The usual arithmetic operations and the most common mathematical functions are supported for complex numbers. For example:

```
void f(complex<float> fl, complex<double> db)
{
    complex<long double> ld {fl+sqrt(db)};
    db += fl*3;
    fl = pow(1/fl,2);
    // ...
}
```

The **sqrt()** and **pow()** (exponentiation) functions are among the usual mathematical functions defined in **<complex>** (§12.2).

12.5 Random Numbers

Random numbers are useful in many contexts, such as testing, games, simulation, and security. The diversity of application areas is reflected in the wide selection of random number generators provided by the standard library in **<random>**. A random number generator consists of two parts:
[1]   an *engine* that produces a sequence of random or pseudo-random values.
[2]   a *distribution* that maps those values into a mathematical distribution in a range.
Examples of distributions are **uniform_int_distribution** (where all integers produced are equally likely), **normal_distribution** ("the bell curve"), and **exponential_distribution** (exponential growth); each for some specified range. For example:

```
using my_engine = default_random_engine;          // type of engine
using my_distribution = uniform_int_distribution<>;  // type of distribution

my_engine re {};                                    // the default engine
my_distribution one_to_six {1,6};                   // distribution that maps to the ints 1..6
auto die = bind(one_to_six,re);                     // make a generator

int x = die();                                      // roll the die: x becomes a value in [1:6]
```

The standard-library function **bind()** makes a function object that will invoke its first argument (here, **one_to_six**) given its second argument (here, **re**) as its argument (§11.5.1). Thus a call **die()** is equivalent to a call **one_to_six(re)**.

Thanks to its uncompromising attention to generality and performance one expert has deemed the standard-library random number component "what every random number library wants to be when it grows up." However, it can hardly be deemed "novice friendly." The **using** statements makes what is being done a bit more obvious. Instead, I could just have written:

```
auto die = bind(uniform_int_distribution<>{1,6}, default_random_engine{});
```

Which version is the more readable depends entirely on the context and the reader.

For novices (of any background) the fully general interface to the random number library can be a serious obstacle. A simple uniform random number generator is often sufficient to get started. For example:

```
Rand_int rnd {1,10};        // make a random number generator for [1:10]
int x = rnd();              // x is a number in [1:10]
```

So, how could we get that? We have to get something like die() inside a class Rand_int:

```
class Rand_int {
public:
    Rand_int(int low, int high) :dist{low,high} { }
    int operator()() { return dist(re); }          // draw an int
private:
    default_random_engine re;
    uniform_int_distribution<> dist;
};
```

That definition is still "expert level," but the *use* of Rand_int() is manageable in the first week of a C++ course for novices. For example:

```
int main()
{
    constexpr int max = 9;
    Rand_int rnd {0,max};                    // make a uniform random number generator

    vector<int> histogram(max+1);            // make a vector of appropriate size
    for (int i=0; i!=200; ++i)
        ++histogram[rnd()];                  // fill histogram with the frequencies of numbers [0:max]

    for (int i = 0; i!=histogram.size(); ++i) {    // write out a bar graph
        cout << i << '\t';
        for (int j=0; j!=histogram[i]; ++j) cout << '*';
        cout << endl;
    }
}
```

The output is a (reassuringly boring) uniform distribution (with reasonable statistical variation):

```
0    *********************
1    ****************
2    ********************
3    *********************
4    *****************
5    ************************
6    ***************************
7    ***********
8    ***********************
9    **************************
```

There is no standard graphics library for C++, so I use "ASCII graphics." Obviously, there are lots of open source and commercial graphics and GUI libraries for C++, but in this book I restrict myself to ISO standard facilities.

12.6 Vector Arithmetic

The vector described in §9.2 was designed to be a general mechanism for holding values, to be flexible, and to fit into the architecture of containers, iterators, and algorithms. However, it does not support mathematical vector operations. Adding such operations to vector would be easy, but its generality and flexibility precludes optimizations that are often considered essential for serious numerical work. Consequently, the standard library provides (in <valarray>) a vector-like template, called valarray, that is less general and more amenable to optimization for numerical computation:

```
template<typename T>
class valarray {
    // ...
};
```

The usual arithmetic operations and the most common mathematical functions are supported for valarrays. For example:

```
void f(valarray<double>& a1, valarray<double>& a2)
{
    valarray<double> a = a1*3.14+a2/a1;        // numeric array operators *, +, /, and =
    a2 += a1*3.14;
    a = abs(a);
    double d = a2[7];
    // ...
}
```

In additions to arithmtic operations, valarray offers stride access to help implement multidimensional computations.

12.7 Numeric Limits

In <limits>, the standard library provides classes that describe the properties of built-in types – such as the maximum exponent of a float or the number of bytes in an int; see §12.7. For example, we can assert that a char is signed:

```
static_assert(numeric_limits<char>::is_signed,"unsigned characters!");
static_assert(100000<numeric_limits<int>::max(),"small ints!");
```

Note that the second assert (only) works because numeric_limits<int>::max() is a constexpr function (§1.7).

12.8 Advice

[1]   The material in this chapter roughly corresponds to what is described in much greater detail in Chapter 40 of [Stroustrup,2013].

[2]   Numerical problems are often subtle. If you are not 100% certain about the mathematical aspects of a numerical problem, either take expert advice, experiment, or do both; §12.1.

[3]   Don't try to do serious numeric computation using only the bare language; use libraries; §12.1.

[4]   Consider **accumulate()**, **inner_product()**, **partial_sum()**, and **adjacent_difference()** before you write a loop to compute a value from a sequence; §12.3.

[5]   Use **std::complex** for complex arithmetic; §12.4.

[6]   Bind an engine to a distribution to get a random number generator; §12.5.

[7]   Be careful that your random numbers are sufficiently random; §12.5.

[8]   Use **valarray** for numeric computation when run-time efficiency is more important than flexibility with respect to operations and element types; §12.6.

[9]   Properties of numeric types are accessible through **numeric_limits**; §12.7.

[10] Use **numeric_limits** to check that the numeric types are adequate for their use; §12.7.

13

Concurrency

Keep it simple:
as simple as possible,
but no simpler.
– A. Einstein

- Introduction
- Tasks and threads
- Passing Arguments
- Returning Results
- Sharing Data
- Waiting for Events
- Communicating Tasks
      future and promise; packaged_task; async()
- Advice

13.1 Introduction

Concurrency – the execution of several tasks simultaneously – is widely used to improve through-put (by using several processors for a single computation) or to improve responsiveness (by allowing one part of a program to progress while another is waiting for a response). All modern programming languages provide support for this. The support provided by the C++ standard library is a portable and type-safe variant of what has been used in C++ for more than 20 years and is almost universally supported by modern hardware. The standard-library support is primarily aimed at supporting systems-level concurrency rather than directly providing sophisticated higher-level concurrency models; those can be supplied as libraries built using the standard-library facilities.

The standard library directly supports concurrent execution of multiple threads in a single address space. To allow that, C++ provides a suitable memory model and a set of atomic operations. The atomic operations allows lock-free programming [Dechev,2010]. The memory model ensures that as long as a programmer avoids data races (uncontrolled concurrent access to mutable data), everything works as one would naively expect. However, most users will see concurrency only in terms of the standard library and libraries built on top of that. This section briefly gives examples of the main standard-library concurrency support facilities: **threads**, **mutex**es, **lock()** operations, **packaged_task**s, and **futures**. These features are built directly upon what operating systems offer and do not incur performance penalties compared with those. Neither do they guarantee significant performance improvements compared to what the operating system offers.

Do not consider concurrency a panacea. If a task can be done sequentially, it is often simpler and faster to do so.

13.2   **Tasks and** threads

We call a computation that can potentially be executed concurrently with other computations a *task*. A *thread* is the system-level representation of a task in a program. A task to be executed concurrently with other tasks is launched by constructing a **std::thread** (found in **<thread>**) with the task as its argument. A task is a function or a function object:

```
void f();                    // function

struct F {                   // function object
     void operator()();      // F's call operator (§5.5)
};

void user()
{
     thread t1 {f};          // f() executes in separate thread
     thread t2 {F()};        // F()() executes in separate thread

     t1.join();              // wait for t1
     t2.join();              // wait for t2
}
```

The **join()**s ensure that we don't exit **user()** until the threads have completed. To "join" a **thread** means to "wait for the thread to terminate."

Threads of a program share a single address space. In this, threads differ from processes, which generally do not directly share data. Since threads share an address space, they can communicate through shared objects (§13.5). Such communication is typically controlled by locks or other mechanisms to prevent data races (uncontrolled concurrent access to a variable).

Programming concurrent tasks can be *very* tricky. Consider possible implementations of the tasks **f** (a function) and **F** (a function object):

```
void f() { cout << "Hello "; }

struct F {
     void operator()() { cout << "Parallel World!\n"; }
};
```

This is an example of a bad error: Here, **f** and **F()** each use the object **cout** without any form of synchronization. The resulting output would be unpredictable and could vary between different executions of the program because the order of execution of the individual operations in the two tasks is not defined. The program may produce "odd" output, such as

PaHeralllel o World!

When defining tasks of a concurrent program, our aim is to keep tasks completely separate except where they communicate in simple and obvious ways. The simplest way of thinking of a concurrent task is as a function that happens to run concurrently with its caller. For that to work, we just have to pass arguments, get a result back, and make sure that there is no use of shared data in between (no data races).

13.3 Passing Arguments

Typically, a task needs data to work upon. We can easily pass data (or pointers or references to the data) as arguments. Consider:

```
void f(vector<double>& v);      // function do something with v

struct F {                      // function object: do something with v
    vector<double>& v;
    F(vector<double>& vv) :v{vv} { }
    void operator()();          // application operator; §5.5
};

int main()
{
    vector<double> some_vec {1,2,3,4,5,6,7,8,9};
    vector<double> vec2 {10,11,12,13,14};

    thread t1 {f,ref(some_vec)};    // f(some_vec) executes in a separate thread
    thread t2 {F{vec2}};            // F(vec2)() executes in a separate thread

    t1.join();
    t2.join();
}
```

Obviously, **F{vec2}** saves a reference to the argument vector in **F**. **F** can now use that vector and hopefully no other task accesses **vec2** while **F** is executing. Passing **vec2** by value would eliminate that risk.

The initialization with **{f,ref(some_vec)}** uses a **thread** variadic template constructor that can accept an arbitrary sequence of arguments (§5.6). The **ref()** is a type function from **<functional>** that unfortunately is needed to tell the variadic template to treat **some_vec** as a reference, rather than as an object. The compiler checks that the first argument can be invoked given the following arguments and builds the necessary function object to pass to the thread. Thus, if **F::operator()()** and **f()** perform the same algorithm, the handling of the two tasks are roughly equivalent: in both cases, a function object is constructed for the **thread** to execute.

13.4   Returning Results

In the example in §13.3, I pass the arguments by non-**const** reference. I only do that if I expect the task to modify the value of the data referred to (§1.8). That's a somewhat sneaky, but not uncommon, way of returning a result. A less obscure technique is to pass the input data by **const** reference and to pass the location of a place to deposit the result as a separate argument:

```
void f(const vector<double>& v, double* res);      // take input from v;  place result in *res

class F {
public:
    F(const vector<double>& vv, double* p) :v{vv}, res{p} { }
    void operator()();              // place result in *res
private:
    const vector<double>& v;        // source of input
    double* res;                    // target for output
};

int main()
{
    vector<double> some_vec;
    vector<double> vec2;
    // ...

    double res1;
    double res2;

    thread t1 {f,cref(some_vec),&res1};      // f(some_vec,&res1) executes in a separate thread
    thread t2 {F{vec2,&res2}};               // F{vec2,&res2}() executes in a separate thread

    t1.join();
    t2.join();

    cout << res1 << ' ' << res2 << '\n';
}
```

This works and the technique is very common, but I don't consider returning results through arguments particularly elegant, so I return to this topic in §13.7.1.

13.5   Sharing Data

Sometimes tasks need to share data. In that case, the access has to be synchronized so that at most one task at a time has access. Experienced programmers will recognize this as a simplification (e.g., there is no problem with many tasks simultaneously reading immutable data), but consider how to ensure that at most one task at a time has access to a given set of objects.

The fundamental element of the solution is a **mutex**, a "mutual exclusion object." A **thread** acquires a mutex using a **lock()** operation:

```
mutex m;  // controlling mutex
int sh;     // shared data

void f()
{
     unique_lock<mutex> lck {m};  // acquire mutex
     sh += 7;                            // manipulate shared data
}  // release mutex implicitly
```

The **unique_lock**'s constructor acquires the mutex (through a call **m.lock()**). If another thread has already acquired the mutex, the thread waits ("blocks") until the other thread completes its access. Once a thread has completed its access to the shared data, the **unique_lock** releases the **mutex** (with a call **m.unlock()**). When a **mutex** is released, **thread**s waiting for it resume executing ("are woken up"). The mutual exclusion and locking facilities are found in **<mutex>**.

The correspondence between the shared data and a **mutex** is conventional: the programmer simply has to know which **mutex** is supposed to correspond to which data. Obviously, this is error-prone, and equally obviously we try to make the correspondence clear through various language means. For example:

```
class Record {
public:
     mutex rm;
     // ...
};
```

It doesn't take a genius to guess that for a **Record** called **rec**, **rec.rm** is a **mutex** that you are supposed to acquire before accessing the other data of **rec**, though a comment or a better name might have helped a reader.

It is not uncommon to need to simultaneously access several resources to perform some action. This can lead to deadlock. For example, if **thread1** acquires **mutex1** and then tries to acquire **mutex2** while **thread2** acquires **mutex2** and then tries to acquire **mutex1**, then neither task will ever proceed further. The standard library offers help in the form of an operation for acquiring several locks simultaneously:

```
void f()
{
     // ...
     unique_lock<mutex> lck1 {m1,defer_lock};   // defer_lock: don't yet try to acquire the mutex
     unique_lock<mutex> lck2 {m2,defer_lock};
     unique_lock<mutex> lck3 {m3,defer_lock};
     // ...
     lock(lck1,lck2,lck3);                             // acquire all three locks
     // ... manipulate shared data ...
} // implicitly release all mutexes
```

This **lock()** will proceed only after acquiring all its **mutex** arguments and will never block ("go to sleep") while holding a **mutex**. The destructors for the individual **unique_lock**s ensure that the **mutex**es are released when a **thread** leaves the scope.

Communicating through shared data is pretty low level. In particular, the programmer has to devise ways of knowing what work has and has not been done by various tasks. In that regard, use of shared data is inferior to the notion of call and return. On the other hand, some people are convinced that sharing must be more efficient than copying arguments and returns. That can indeed be so when large amounts of data are involved, but locking and unlocking are relatively expensive operations. On the other hand, modern machines are very good at copying data, especially compact data, such as **vector** elements. So don't choose shared data for communication because of "efficiency" without thought and preferably not without measurement.

13.6 Waiting for Events

Sometimes, a **thread** needs to wait for some kind of external event, such as another **thread** completing a task or a certain amount of time having passed. The simplest "event" is simply time passing. Using the time facilities found in **<chrono>** I can write:

```
using namespace std::chrono;        // see §11.4

auto t0 = high_resolution_clock::now();
this_thread::sleep_for(milliseconds{20});
auto t1 = high_resolution_clock::now();

cout << duration_cast<nanoseconds>(t1–t0).count() << " nanoseconds passed\n";
```

Note that I didn't even have to launch a **thread**; by default, **this_thread** refers to the one and only thread.

I used **duration_cast** to adjust the clock's units to the nanoseconds I wanted.

The basic support for communicating using external events is provided by **condition_variables** found in **<condition_variable>**. A **condition_variable** is a mechanism allowing one **thread** to wait for another. In particular, it allows a **thread** to wait for some *condition* (often called an *event*) to occur as the result of work done by other **threads**.

Using **condition_variables** supports many forms of elegant and efficient sharing, but can be rather tricky. Consider the classical example of two **threads** communicating by passing messages through a **queue**. For simplicity, I declare the **queue** and the mechanism for avoiding race conditions on that **queue** global to the producer and consumer:

```
class Message {      // object to be communicated
    // ...
};
```

```
queue<Message> mqueue;          // the queue of messages
condition_variable mcond;       // the variable communicating events
mutex mmutex;                   // the locking mechanism
```

The types **queue**, **condition_variable**, and **mutex** are provided by the standard library.

The **consumer()** reads and processes **Messages**:

```
void consumer()
{
    while(true) {
        unique_lock<mutex> lck{mmutex};      // acquire mmutex
        mcond.wait(lck));                     // release lck and wait;
                                              // re-acquire lck upon wakeup

        auto m = mqueue.front();              // get the message
        mqueue.pop();
        lck.unlock();                         // release lck
        // ... process m ...
    }
}
```

Here, I explicitly protect the operations on the `queue` and on the `condition_variable` with a `unique_lock` on the `mutex`. Waiting on `condition_variable` releases its lock argument until the wait is over (so that the queue is non-empty) and then reacquires it.

The corresponding `producer` looks like this:

```
void producer()
{
    while(true) {
        Message m;
        // ... fill the message ...
        unique_lock<mutex> lck {mmutex};      // protect operations
        mqueue.push(m);
        mcond.notify_one();                   // notify
    }                                         // release lock (at end of scope)
}
```

13.7 Communicating Tasks

The standard library provides a few facilities to allow programmers to operate at the conceptual level of tasks (work to potentially be done concurrently) rather than directly at the lower level of threads and locks:

[1] `future` and `promise` for returning a value from a task spawned on a separate thread

[2] `packaged_task` to help launch tasks and connect up the mechanisms for returning a result

[3] `async()` for launching of a task in a manner very similar to calling a function.

These facilities are found in `<future>`.

13.7.1 future and promise

The important point about `future` and `promise` is that they enable a transfer of a value between two tasks without explicit use of a lock; "the system" implements the transfer efficiently. The basic idea is simple: When a task wants to pass a value to another, it puts the value into a `promise`. Somehow, the implementation makes that value appear in the corresponding `future`, from which it can be read (typically by the launcher of the task). We can represent this graphically:

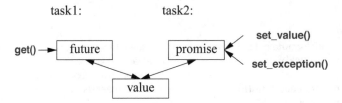

If we have a **future<X>** called **fx**, we can **get()** a value of type **X** from it:

>   X v = fx.get();   // if necessary, wait for the value to get computed

If the value isn't there yet, our thread is blocked until it arrives. If the value couldn't be computed, **get()** might throw an exception (from the system or transmitted from the task from which we were trying to **get()** the value).

The main purpose of a **promise** is to provide simple "put" operations (called **set_value()** and **set_exception()**) to match **future**'s **get()**. The names "future" and "promise" are historical; please don't blame or credit me. They are yet another fertile source of puns.

If you have a **promise** and need to send a result of type **X** to a **future**, you can do one of two things: pass a value or pass an exception. For example:

```
void f(promise<X>& px)  // a task: place the result in px
{
    // ...
    try {
        X res;
        // ... compute a value for res ...
        px.set_value(res);
    }
    catch (...) {         // oops: couldn't compute res
        px.set_exception(current_exception());      // pass the exception to the future's thread
    }
}
```

The **current_exception()** refers to the caught exception.

To deal with an exception transmitted through a **future**, the caller of **get()** must be prepared to catch it somewhere. For example:

```
void g(future<X>& fx)          // a task: get the result from fx
{
    // ...
    try {
        X v = fx.get();  // if necessary, wait for the value to get computed
        // ... use v ...
    }
    catch (...) {          // oops: someone couldn't compute v
        // ... handle error ...
    }
}
```

If the error doesn't need to be handled by **g()** itself, the code reduces to the minimal:

```
void g(future<X>& fx)          // a task: get the result from fx
{
    // ...
    X v = fx.get();   // if necessary, wait for the value to get computed
    // ... use v ...
}
```

13.7.2 packaged_task

How do we get a **future** into the task that needs a result and the corresponding **promise** into the thread that should produce that result? The **packaged_task** type is provided to simplify setting up tasks connected with **futures** and **promises** to be run on **threads**. A **packaged_task** provides wrapper code to put the return value or exception from the task into a **promise** (like the code shown in §13.7.1). If you ask it by calling **get_future**, a **packaged_task** will give you the **future** corresponding to its **promise**. For example, we can set up two tasks to each add half of the elements of a **vector<double>** using the standard-library **accumulate()** (§12.3):

```
double accum(double* beg, double* end, double init)
    // compute the sum of [beg:end) starting with the initial value init
{
    return accumulate(beg,end,init);
}

double comp2(vector<double>& v)
{
    using Task_type = double(double*,double*,double);          // type of task

    packaged_task<Task_type> pt0 {accum};                      // package the task (i.e., accum)
    packaged_task<Task_type> pt1 {accum};

    future<double> f0 {pt0.get_future()};                      // get hold of pt0's future
    future<double> f1 {pt1.get_future()};                      // get hold of pt1's future

    double* first = &v[0];
    thread t1 {move(pt0),first,first+v.size()/2,0};            // start a thread for pt0
    thread t2 {move(pt1),first+v.size()/2,first+v.size(),0};   // start a thread for pt1

    // ...

    return f0.get()+f1.get();                                  // get the results
}
```

The **packaged_task** template takes the type of the task as its template argument (here **Task_type**, an alias for **double(double*,double*,double)**) and the task as its constructor argument (here, **accum**). The **move()** operations are needed because a **packaged_task** cannot be copied. The reason that a **packaged_task** cannot be copied is that it is a resource handle: it owns its **promise** and is (indirectly) responsible for whatever resoures its task may own.

Please note the absence of explicit mention of locks in this code: we are able to concentrate on tasks to be done, rather than on the mechanisms used to manage their communication. The two tasks will be run on separate threads and thus potentially in parallel.

13.7.3 async()

The line of thinking I have pursued in this chapter is the one I believe to be the simplest yet still among the most powerful: Treat a task as a function that may happen to run concurrently with other tasks. It is far from the only model supported by the C++ standard library, but it serves well for a wide range of needs. More subtle and tricky models, e.g., styles of programming relying on shared memory, can be used as needed.

To launch tasks to potentially run asynchronously, we can use **async()**:

```
double comp4(vector<double>& v)
     // spawn many tasks if v is large enough
{
     if (v.size()<10000)          // is it worth using concurrency?
          return accum(v.begin(),v.end(),0.0);

     auto v0 = &v[0];
     auto sz = v.size();

     auto f0 = async(accum,v0,v0+sz/4,0.0);          // first quarter
     auto f1 = async(accum,v0+sz/4,v0+sz/2,0.0);     // second quarter
     auto f2 = async(accum,v0+sz/2,v0+sz*3/4,0.0);   // third quarter
     auto f3 = async(accum,v0+sz*3/4,v0+sz,0.0);     // fourth quarter

     return f0.get()+f1.get()+f2.get()+f3.get();  // collect and combine the results
}
```

Basically, **async()** separates the "call part" of a function call from the "get the result part," and separates both from the actual execution of the task. Using **async()**, you don't have to think about threads and locks. Instead, you think just in terms of tasks that potentially compute their results asynchronously. There is an obvious limitation: Don't even think of using **async()** for tasks that share resources needing locking – with **async()** you don't even know how many **thread**s will be used because that's up to **async()** to decide based on what it knows about the system resources available at the time of a call. For example, **async()** may check whether any idle cores (processors) are available before deciding how many **thread**s to use.

Using a guess about the cost of computation relative to the cost of launching a **thread**, such as **v.size()<10000**, is very primitive and prone to gross mistakes about performance. However, this is not the place for a proper disussion about how to manage **thread**s. Don't take this estimate as more than a simple and probably poor guess.

Please note that **async()** is not just a mechanism specialized for parallel computation for increased performance. For example, it can also be used to spawn a task for getting information from a user, leaving the "main program" active with something else (§13.7.3).

13.8 Advice

[1]   The material in this chapter roughly corresponds to what is described in much greater detail in Chapters 41-42 of [Stroustrup,2013].

[2]   Use concurrency to improve responsiveness or to improve throughput; §13.1.

[3]   Work at the highest level of abstraction that you can afford; §13.1.

[4]   Consider processes as an alternative to threads; §13.1.

[5]   The standard-library concurrency facilities are type safe; §13.1.

[6]   The memory model exists to save most programmers from having to think about the machine architecture level of computers; §13.1.

[7]   The memory model makes memory appear roughly as naively expected; §13.1.

[8]   Atomics allow for lock-free programming; §13.1.

[9]   Leave lock-free programming to experts; §13.1.

[10]   Sometimes, a sequential solution is simpler and faster than a concurrent solution; §13.1.

[11]   Avoid data races; §13.1, §13.2.

[12]   A **thread** is a type-safe interface to a system thread; §13.2.

[13]   Use **join()** to wait for a **thread** to complete; §13.2.

[14]   Avoid explicitly shared data whenever you can; §13.2.

[15]   Use **unique_lock** to manage mutexes; §13.5.

[16]   Use **lock()** to acquire multiple locks; §13.5.

[17]   Use **condition_variable**s to manage communication among **thread**s; §13.6.

[18]   Think in terms of tasks that can be executed concurrently, rather than directly in terms of **thread**s; §13.7.

[19]   Value simplicity; §13.7.

[20]   Prefer **packaged_task** and **future**s over direct use of **thread**s and **mutex**es; §13.7.

[21]   Return a result using a **promise** and get a result from a **future**; §13.7.1.

[22]   Use **packaged_task**s to handle exceptions thrown by tasks and to arrange for value return; §13.7.2.

[23]   Use a **packaged_task** and a **future** to express a request to an external service and wait for its response; §13.7.2.

[24]   Use **async()** to launch simple tasks; §13.7.3.

14

History and Compatibility

Hurry Slowly
(festina lente).
– *Octavius, Caesar Augustus*

- History
    Timeline; The Early Years; The ISO C++ Standards
- C++11 Extensions
    Language Features; Standard-Library Components; Deprecated Features; Casts
- C/C++ Compatibility
    C and C++ Are Siblings; Compatibility Problems
- Bibliography
- Advice

14.1 History

I invented C++, wrote its early definitions, and produced its first implementation. I chose and formulated the design criteria for C++, designed its major language features, developed or helped to develop many of the early libraries, and was responsible for the processing of extension proposals in the C++ standards committee.

C++ was designed to provide Simula's facilities for program organization [Dahl,1970] together with C's efficiency and flexibility for systems programming [Kernighan,1978]. Simula is the initial source of C++'s abstraction mechanisms. The class concept (with derived classes and virtual functions) was borrowed from it. However, templates and exceptions came to C++ later with different sources of inspiration.

The evolution of C++ was always in the context of its use. I spent a lot of time listening to users and seeking out the opinions of experienced programmers. In particular, my colleagues at AT&T Bell Laboratories were essential for the growth of C++ during its first decade.

This section is a brief overview; it does not try to mention every language feature and library component. Furthermore, it does not go into details. For more information, and in particular for more names of people who contributed, see [Stroustrup,1993], [Stroustrup,2007], and [Stroustrup,1994]. My two papers from the ACM History of Programming Languages conference and my *Design and Evolution of C++* book (known as "D&E") describe the design and evolution of C++ in detail and document influences from other programming languages.

Most of the documents produced as part of the ISO C++ standards effort are available online [WG21]. In my FAQ, I try to maintain a connection between the standard facilities and the people who proposed and refined those facilities [Stroustrup,2010]. C++ is not the work of a faceless, anonymous committee or of a supposedly omnipotent "dictator for life"; it is the work of many dedicated, experienced, hard-working individuals.

14.1.1 Timeline

The work that led to C++ started in the fall of 1979 under the name "C with Classes." Here is a simplified timeline:

1979 Work on "C with Classes" started. The initial feature set included classes and derived classes, public/private access control, constructors and destructors, and function declarations with argument checking. The first library supported non-preemptive concurrent tasks and random number generators.

1984 "C with Classes" was renamed to C++. By then, C++ had acquired virtual functions, function and operator overloading, references, and the I/O stream and complex number libraries.

1985 First commercial release of C++ (October 14). The library included I/O streams, complex numbers, and tasks (non-preemptive scheduling).

1985 *The C++ Programming Language* ("TC++PL," October 14) [Stroustrup,1986].

1989 *The Annotated C++ Reference Manual* ("the ARM") [Ellis,1989].

1991 *The C++ Programming Language, Second Edition* [Stroustrup,1991], presenting generic programming using templates and error handling based on exceptions (including the "Resource Acquisition Is Initialization" general resource management idiom).

1997 *The C++ Programming Language, Third Edition* [Stroustrup,1997] introduced ISO C++, including namespaces, **dynamic_cast**, and many refinements of templates. The standard library added the STL framework of generic containers and algorithms.

1998 ISO C++ standard [C++,1998].

2002 Work on a revised standard, colloquially named C++0x, started.

2003 A "bug fix" revision of the ISO C++ standard was issued. A C++ Technical Report introduced new standard-library components, such as regular expressions, unordered containers (hash tables), and resource management pointers, which later became part of C++0x.

2006 An ISO C++ Technical Report on Performance was issued to answer questions of cost, predictability, and techniques, mostly related to embedded systems programming [C++,2004].

2009 C++0x was feature complete. It provided uniform initialization, move semantics, variadic template arguments, lambda expressions, type aliases, a memory model suitable for concurrency, and much more. The standard library added several components, including threads, locks, and most of the components from the 2003 Technical Report.

2011 ISO C++11 standard was formally approved [C++,2011].

2012 Work on future ISO C++ standards (referred to as C++14 and C++17) started.

2013 The first complete C++11 implementations emerged.

2013 *The C++ Programming Language, Fourth Edition* introduced C++11.

During development, C++11 was known as C++0x. As is not uncommon in large projects, we were overly optimistic about the completion date.

14.1.2 The Early Years

I originally designed and implemented the language because I wanted to distribute the services of a UNIX kernel across multiprocessors and local-area networks (what are now known as multicores and clusters). For that, I needed some event-driven simulations for which Simula would have been ideal, except for performance considerations. I also needed to deal directly with hardware and provide high-performance concurrent programming mechanisms for which C would have been ideal, except for its weak support for modularity and type checking. The result of adding Simula-style classes to C (Classic C; §14.3.1), "C with Classes," was used for major projects in which its facilities for writing programs that use minimal time and space were severely tested. It lacked operator overloading, references, virtual functions, templates, exceptions, and many, many details [Stroustrup,1982]. The first use of C++ outside a research organization started in July 1983.

The name C++ (pronounced "see plus plus") was coined by Rick Mascitti in the summer of 1983 and chosen as the replacement for "C with Classes" by me. The name signifies the evolutionary nature of the changes from C; "++" is the C increment operator. The slightly shorter name "C+" is a syntax error; it had also been used as the name of an unrelated language. Connoisseurs of C semantics find C++ inferior to ++C. The language was not called D, because it was an extension of C, because it did not attempt to remedy problems by removing features, and because there already existed several would-be C successors named D. For yet another interpretation of the name C++, see the appendix of [Orwell,1949].

C++ was designed primarily so that my friends and I would not have to program in assembler, C, or various then-fashionable high-level languages. Its main purpose was to make writing good programs easier and more pleasant for the individual programmer. In the early years, there was no C++ paper design; design, documentation, and implementation went on simultaneously. There was no "C++ project" either, or a "C++ design committee." Throughout, C++ evolved to cope with problems encountered by users and as a result of discussions among my friends, my colleagues, and me.

The very first design of C++ (then called "C with Classes") included function declarations with argument type checking and implicit conversions, classes with the **public/private** distinction between the interface and the implementation, derived classes, and constructors and destructors. I used macros to provide primitive parameterization. This was in non-experimental use by mid-1980. Late that year, I was able to present a set of language facilities supporting a coherent set of programming styles. In retrospect, I consider the introduction of constructors and destructors most significant. In the terminology of the time, "a constructor creates the execution environment for the member functions and the destructor reverses that." Here is the root of C++'s strategies for resource management (causing a demand for exceptions) and the key to many techniques for making user code short and clear. If there were other languages at the time that supported multiple constructors capable of executing general code, I didn't (and don't) know of them. Destructors were new in C++.

C++ was released commercially in October 1985. By then, I had added inlining (§1.4, §4.2.1), consts (§1.7), function overloading (§1.4), references (§1.8), operator overloading (§4.2.1), and virtual functions (§4.4). Of these features, support for run-time polymorphism in the form of virtual functions was by far the most controversial. I knew its worth from Simula but found it impossible to convince most people in the systems programming world of its value. Systems programmers tended to view indirect function calls with suspicion, and people acquainted with other languages supporting object-oriented programming had a hard time believing that virtual functions could be fast enough to be useful in systems code. Conversely, many programmers with an object-oriented background had (and many still have) a hard time getting used to the idea that you use virtual function calls only to express a choice that must be made at run time. The resistance to virtual functions may be related to a resistance to the idea that you can get better systems through more regular structure of code supported by a programming language. Many C programmers seem convinced that what really matters is complete flexibility and careful individual crafting of every detail of a program. My view was (and is) that we need every bit of help we can get from languages and tools: the inherent complexity of the systems we are trying to build is always at the edge of what we can express.

Much of the design of C++ was done on the blackboards of my colleagues. In the early years, the feedback from Stu Feldman, Alexander Fraser, Steve Johnson, Brian Kernighan, Doug McIlroy, and Dennis Ritchie was invaluable.

In the second half of the 1980s, I continued to add language features in response to user comments. The most important of those were templates [Stroustrup,1988] and exception handling [Koenig,1990], which were considered experimental at the time the standards effort started. In the design of templates, I was forced to decide among flexibility, efficiency, and early type checking. At the time, nobody knew how to simultaneously get all three. To compete with C-style code for demanding systems applications, I felt that I had to choose the first two properties. In retrospect, I think the choice was the correct one, and the search for better type checking of templates continues [DosReis,2006] [Gregor,2006] [Sutton,2011] [Stroustrup,2012a]. The design of exceptions focused on multilevel propagation of exceptions, the passing of arbitrary information to an error handler, and the integration between exceptions and resource management by using local objects with destructors to represent and release resources (what I clumsily called *Resource Acquisition Is Initialization*; §4.2.2).

I generalized C++'s inheritance mechanisms to support multiple base classes [Stroustrup,1987a]. This was called *multiple inheritance* and was considered difficult and controversial. I considered it far less important than templates or exceptions. Multiple inheritance of abstract classes (often called *interfaces*) is now universal in languages supporting static type checking and object-oriented programming.

The C++ language evolved hand in hand with some of the key library facilities presented in this book. For example, I designed the complex [Stroustrup,1984], vector, stack, and (I/O) stream [Stroustrup,1985] classes together with the operator overloading mechanisms. The first string and list classes were developed by Jonathan Shopiro and me as part of the same effort. Jonathan's string and list classes were the first to see extensive use as part of a library. The string class from the standard C++ library has its roots in these early efforts. The task library described in [Stroustrup,1987b] was part of the first "C with Classes" program ever written in 1980. I wrote it and its associated classes to support Simula-style simulations. Unfortunately, we had to wait until 2011 (30 years!) to get concurrency support standardized and universally available (Chapter 13). The development of the template facility was influenced by a variety of **vector**, **map**, **list**, and **sort** templates devised by Andrew Koenig, Alex Stepanov, me, and others.

The most important innovation in the 1998 standard library was the inclusion of the STL, a framework of algorithms and containers, in the standard library (Chapter 9, Chapter 10). It was the work of Alex Stepanov (with Dave Musser, Meng Lee, and others) based on more than a decade's work on generic programming. The STL has been massively influential within the C++ community and beyond.

C++ grew up in an environment with a multitude of established and experimental programming languages (e.g., Ada [Ichbiah,1979], Algol 68 [Woodward,1974], and ML [Paulson,1996]). At the time, I was comfortable in about 25 languages, and their influences on C++ are documented in [Stroustrup,1994] and [Stroustrup,2007]. However, the determining influences always came from the applications I encountered. That was a deliberate policy to have the development of C++ "problem driven" rather than imitative.

14.1.3 The ISO C++ Standards

The explosive growth of C++ use caused some changes. Sometime during 1987, it became clear that formal standardization of C++ was inevitable and that we needed to start preparing the ground for a standardization effort [Stroustrup,1994]. The result was a conscious effort to maintain contact between implementers of C++ compilers and major users. This was done through paper and electronic mail and through face-to-face meetings at C++ conferences and elsewhere.

AT&T Bell Labs made a major contribution to C++ and its wider community by allowing me to share drafts of revised versions of the C++ reference manual with implementers and users. Because many of those people worked for companies that could be seen as competing with AT&T, the significance of this contribution should not be underestimated. A less enlightened company could have caused major problems of language fragmentation simply by doing nothing. As it happened, about a hundred individuals from dozens of organizations read and commented on what became the generally accepted reference manual and the base document for the ANSI C++ standardization effort. Their names can be found in *The Annotated C++ Reference Manual* ("the ARM") [Ellis,1989]. The X3J16 committee of ANSI was convened in December 1989 at the initiative of Hewlett-Packard. In June 1991, this ANSI (American national) standardization of C++ became part of an ISO (international) standardization effort for C++ and named WG21. From 1990, these joint C++ standards committees have been the main forum for the evolution of C++ and the refinement of its definition. I served on these committees throughout. In particular, as the chairman of the working group for extensions (later called the evolution group), I was directly responsible for handling proposals for major changes to C++ and the addition of new language features. An initial draft standard for public review was produced in April 1995. The first ISO C++ standard (ISO/IEC 14882-1998) [C++,1998] was ratified by a 22-0 national vote in 1998. A "bug fix release" of this standard was issued in 2003, so you sometimes hear people refer to C++03, but that is essentially the same language as C++98.

The current C++, C++11, known for years as C++0x, is the work of the members of WG21. The committee worked under increasingly onerous self-imposed processes and procedures. These processes probably led to a better (and more rigorous) specification, but they also limited innovation [Stroustrup,2007]. An initial draft standard for public review was produced in 2009. The second ISO C++ standard (ISO/IEC 14882-2011) [C++,2011] was ratified by a 21-0 national vote in August 2011.

One reason for the long gap between the two standards is that most members of the committee (including me) were under the mistaken impression that the ISO rules required a "waiting period" after a standard was issued before starting work on new features. Consequently, serious work on new language features did not start until 2002. Other reasons included the increased size of modern languages and their foundation libraries. In terms of pages of standards text, the language grew by about 30% and the standard library by about 100%. Much of the increase was due to more detailed specification, rather than new functionality. Also, the work on a new C++ standard obviously had to take great care not to compromise older code through incompatible changes. There are billions of lines of C++ code in use that the committee must not break.

C++11 added massively to the standard library and pushed to complete the feature set needed for a programming style that is a synthesis of the "paradigms" and idioms that have proven successful with C++98. The overall aims for the C++11 effort were:

- Make C++ a better language for systems programming and library building.
- Make C++ easier to teach and learn.

The aims are documented and detailed in [Stroustrup,2007].

A major effort was made to make concurrent systems programming type-safe and portable. This involved a memory model (§13.1) and a set of facilities for lock-free programming, which is primarily the work of Hans Boehm, Brian McKnight, and others. On top of that, we added the **threads** library.

14.2 C++11 Extensions

Here, I list the language features and standard-library components that have been added to C++ for the C++11 standard.

14.2.1 Language Features

Looking at a list of language features can be quite bewildering. Remember that a language feature is not meant to be used in isolation. In particular, most features that are new in C++11 make no sense in isolation from the framework provided by older features.

[1]   Uniform and general initialization using {}-lists (§1.5, §4.2.3)
[2]   Type deduction from initializer: **auto** (§1.5)
[3]   Prevention of narrowing (§1.5)
[4]   Generalized and guaranteed constant expressions: **constexpr** (§1.7)
[5]   Range-**for**-statement (§1.8)
[6]   Null pointer keyword: **nullptr** (§1.8)

[7]   Scoped and strongly typed **enums: enum class** (§2.5)
[8]   Compile-time assertions: **static_assert** (§3.4.3)
[9]   Language mapping of {}-list to **std::initializer_list** (§4.2.3)
[10]   Rvalue references (enabling move semantics; §4.6.2)
[11]   Nested template arguments ending with **>>** (no space between the **>**s)
[12]   Lambdas (§5.5)
[13]   Variadic templates (§5.6)
[14]   Type and template aliases (§5.7)
[15]   Unicode characters
[16]   **long long** integer type
[17]   Alignment controls: **alignas** and **alignof**
[18]   The ability to use the type of an expression as a type in a declaration: **decltype**
[19]   Raw string literals (§7.3)
[20]   Generalized POD ("Plain Old Data")
[21]   Generalized **unions**
[22]   Local classes as template arguments
[23]   Suffix return type syntax
[24]   A syntax for attributes and two standard attributes: **[[carries_dependency]]** and **[[noreturn]]**
[25]   Preventing exception propagation: the **noexcept** specifier (§3.4.1)
[26]   Testing for the possibility of a **throw** in an expression: the **noexcept** operator.
[27]   C99 features: extended integral types (i.e., rules for optional longer integer types); con-
       catenation of narrow/wide strings; **__STDC_HOSTED__**; **_Pragma(X)**; vararg macros and
       empty macro arguments
[28]   **__func__** as the name of a string holding the name of the current function
[29]   **inline** namespaces
[30]   Delegating constructors
[31]   In-class member initializers
[32]   Control of defaults: **default** and **delete** (§4.6.5)
[33]   Explicit conversion operators
[34]   User-defined literals
[35]   More explicit control of **template** instantiation: **extern templates**
[36]   Default template arguments for function templates
[37]   Inheriting constructors
[38]   Override controls: **override** and **final** (§4.5.1)
[39]   A simpler and more general SFINAE (Substitution Failure Is Not An Error) rule
[40]   Memory model (§13.1)
[41]   Thread-local storage: **thread_local**

For a more complete description of the changes to C++98 in C++11, see [Stroustrup,2013].

14.2.2 Standard-Library Components

The C++11 additions to the standard library come in two forms: new components (such as the regular expression matching library) and improvements to C++98 components (such as move constructors for containers).

[1]   initializer_list constructors for containers (§4.2.3)
[2]   Move semantics for containers (§4.6.2, §9.2)
[3]   A singly-linked list: forward_list (§9.6)
[4]   Hash containers: unordered_map, unordered_multimap, unordered_set, and unordered_multiset (§9.6, §9.5)
[5]   Resource management pointers: unique_ptr, shared_ptr, and weak_ptr (§11.2.1)
[6]   Concurrency support: thread (§13.2), mutexes (§13.5), locks (§13.5), and condition variables (§13.6)
[7]   Higher-level concurrency support: packaged_thread, future, promise, and async() (§13.7)
[8]   tuples (§11.3.3)
[9]   Regular expressions: regex (§7.3)
[10]   Random numbers: uniform_int_distribution, normal_distribution, random_engine, etc. (§12.5)
[11]   Integer type names, such as int16_t, uint32_t, and int_fast64_t
[12]   A fixed-sized contiguous sequence container: array (§11.3.1)
[13]   Copying and rethrowing exceptions (§13.7.1)
[14]   Error reporting using error codes: system_error
[15]   emplace() operations for containers
[16]   Wide use of constexpr functions
[17]   Systematic use of noexcept functions
[18]   Improved function adaptors: function and bind() (§11.5)
[19]   string to numeric value conversions
[20]   Scoped allocators
[21]   Type traits, such as is_integral and is_base_of (§11.6.2)
[22]   Time utilities: duration and time_point (§11.4)
[23]   Compile-time rational arithmetic: ratio
[24]   Abandoning a process: quick_exit
[25]   More algorithms, such as move(), copy_if(), and is_sorted() (Chapter 10)
[26]   Garbage collection ABI (§4.6.4)
[27]   Low-level concurrency support: atomics

14.2.3 Deprecated Features

By deprecating a feature, the standards committee expresses the wish that the feature will go away. However, the committee does not have a mandate to immediately remove a heavily used feature – however redundant or dangerous it may be. Thus, a deprecation is a strong hint to avoid the feature. It may disappear in the future. Compilers are likely to issue warnings for uses of deprecated features. However, deprecated features are part of the standard and history shows that unfortunately they tend to remain supported "forever" for reasons of compatibility.

• Generation of the copy constructor and the copy assignment is deprecated for a class with a destructor.
• It is no longer allowed to assign a string literal to a char*. Instead of char* as a target for assignment and initializations with string literals, use const char* or auto.

- C++98 exception specifications are deprecated:

  void f() throw(X,Y);   *// C++98; now deprecated*

  The support facilities for exception specifications, **unexcepted_handler**, **set_unexpected()**, **get_unexpected()**, and **unexpected()**, are similarly deprecated. Instead, use **noexcept** (§3.4.1).
- Some C++ standard-library function objects and associated functions are deprecated. Most relate to argument binding. Instead use lambdas, **bind**, and **function** (§11.5).
- The **auto_ptr** is deprecated. Instead, use **unique_ptr** (§11.2.1).
- The use of the storage specifier **register** is deprecated.
- The use of **++** on a **bool** is deprecated.

In addition, the committee did remove the essentially unused **export** feature, because it was complex and not shipped by the major vendors.

14.2.4 Casts

C-style casts should have been deprecated in favor of *named casts*. The named casts are:
- **static_cast**: for reasonably well-behaved conversions, such as from a pointer to a base to its derived class.
- **reinterpret_cast**: For really nasty, non-portable conversions, such as conversion of an **int** to a pointer type.
- **const_cast**: For casting away **const**.

For example:

```
Widget* pw = static_cast<Widget*>(pv);          // pv is a void* supposed to point to a Widget
auto dd = reintrepret_cast<Device_driver*>(0xFF00);   // 0xFF00 is supposed to point to a device driver
char* pc = const_cast<char*>("Casts are inherently dangerous");
```

A literal starting with **0x** is a hexadecimal (base 16) integer.

Programmers should seriously consider banning C-style casts from their own programs. Where explicit type conversion is necessary, a combination of named casts can do what a C-style cast can. The named casts should be preferred because they are more explicit and more visible.

Explicit type conversion can be completely avoided in most high-level code, so consider every cast (however expressed) a blemish on your design. Consider defining a function **narrow_cast<T>(v)** that checks if the value **v** can be represented as a **T** without loss of information (without *narrowing*) and throws an exception if it cannot. For class hierarchy navigation, prefer the checked **dynamic_cast** (§4.5.3).

14.3 C/C++ Compatibility

With minor exceptions, C++ is a superset of C (meaning C11; [C11]). Most differences stem from C++'s greater emphasis on type checking. Well-written C programs tend to be C++ programs as well. A compiler can diagnose every difference between C++ and C. The C99/C++11 incompatibilities are listed in §iso.C. At the time of writing, C11 is still very new and most C code is Classic C or C99 [C99].

14.3.1 C and C++ Are Siblings

Classic C has two main descendants: ISO C and ISO C++. Over the years, these languages have evolved at different paces and in different directions. One result of this is that each language provides support for traditional C-style programming in slightly different ways. The resulting incompatibilities can make life miserable for people who use both C and C++, for people who write in one language using libraries implemented in the other, and for implementers of libraries and tools for C and C++.

How can I call C and C++ siblings? Clearly, C++ is a descendant of C. However, look at a simplified family tree:

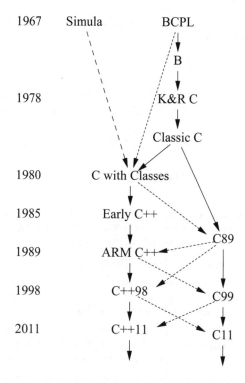

A solid line means a massive inheritance of features, a dashed line a borrowing of major features, and a dotted line a borrowing of minor features. From this, ISO C and ISO C++ emerge as the two major descendants of K&R C [Kernighan,1978], and as siblings. Each carries with it the key aspects of Classic C, and neither is 100% compatible with Classic C. I picked the term "Classic C" from a sticker that used to be affixed to Dennis Ritchie's terminal. It is K&R C plus enumerations and **struct** assignment. BCPL is defined by [Richards,1980] and C89 by [C1990].

Incompatibilities are nasty for programmers in part because they create a combinatorial explosion of alternatives. Consider a simple Venn diagram:

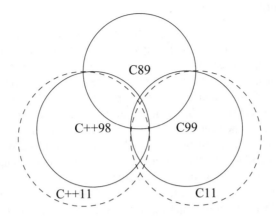

The areas are not to scale. Both C++11 and C11 have most of K&R C as a subset. C++11 has most of C11 as a subset. There are features belonging to most of the distinct areas. For example:

C89 only	Call of undeclared function
C99 only	Variable-length arrays (VLAs)
C++ only	Templates
C89 and C99	Algol-style function definitions
C89 and C++	Use of the C99 keyword restrict as an identifier
C++ and C99	// comments
C89, C++, and C99	structs
C++11 only	Move semantics (using rvalue references; &&)
C11 only	Type-generic expressions using the _Generic keyword
C++11 and C11	Atomics

Note that differences between C and C++ are not necessarily the result of changes to C made in C++. In several cases, the incompatibilities arise from features adopted incompatibly into C long after they were common in C++. Examples are the ability to assign a T* to a void* and the linkage of global consts [Stroustrup,2002]. Sometimes, a feature was even incompatibly adopted into C after it was part of the ISO C++ standard, such as details of the meaning of inline.

14.3.2 Compatibility Problems

There are many minor incompatibilities between C and C++. All can cause problems for a programmer, but all can be coped with in the context of C++. If nothing else, C code fragments can be compiled as C and linked to using the extern "C" mechanism.

The major problems for converting a C program to C++ are likely to be:

- Suboptimal design and programming style.
- A void* implicitly converted to a T* (that is, converted without a cast).
- C++ keywords used as identifiers in C code.
- Incompatible linkage between code fragments compiled as C and code fragments compiled as C++.

14.3.2.1 Style Problems

Natually, a C program is written in a C style, such as the style used in K&R [Kernighan,1988]. This implies widespread use of pointers and arrays, and probably many macros. These facilities are hard to use reliably in a large program. Resource management and error handling are often ad hoc, documented (rather than language and tool supported), and often incompletely documented and adhered to. A simple line-for-line conversion of a C program into a C++ program yields a program that is often a bit better checked. In fact, I have never converted a C program into C++ without finding some bug. However, the fundamental structure is unchanged, and so are the fundamental sources of errors. If you had incomplete error handling, resource leaks, or buffer overflows in the original C program, they will still be there in the C++ version. To obtain major benefits, you must make changes to the fundamental structure of the code:

[1]   Don't think of C++ as C with a few features added. C++ can be used that way, but only suboptimally. To get really major advantages from C++ as compared to C, you need to apply different design and implementation styles.

[2]   Use the C++ standard library as a teacher of new techniques and programming styles. Note the difference from the C standard library (e.g., = rather than strcpy() for copying and == rather than strcmp() for comparing).

[3]   Macro substitution is almost never necessary in C++. Use const (§1.7), constexpr (§1.7), enum or enum class (§2.5) to define manifest constants, inline (§4.2.1) to avoid function-calling overhead, templates (Chapter 5) to specify families of functions and types, and namespaces (§3.3) to avoid name clashes.

[4]   Don't declare a variable before you need it, and initialize it immediately. A declaration can occur anywhere a statement can (§1.9), in for-statement initializers (§1.8), and in conditions (§4.5.3).

[5]   Don't use malloc(). The new operator (§4.2.2) does the same job better, and instead of realloc(), try a vector (§4.2.3, §10.1). Don't just replace malloc() and free() with "naked" new and delete (§4.2.2).

[6]   Avoid void*, unions, and casts, except deep within the implementation of some function or class. Their use limits the support you can get from the type system and can harm performance. In most cases, a cast is an indication of a design error.

[7]   If you must use an explicit type conversion, use an appropriate named cast (e.g., static_cast; §14.2.3) for a more precise statement of what you are trying to do.

[8]   Minimize the use of arrays and C-style strings. C++ standard-library strings (§7.2), arrays (§11.3.1), and vectors (§9.2) can often be used to write simpler and more maintainable code compared to the traditional C style. In general, try not to build yourself what has already been provided by the standard library.

[9]   Avoid pointer arithmetic except in very specialized code (such as a memory manager) and for simple array traversal (e.g., ++p).

[10] Do not assume that something laboriously written in C style (avoiding C++ features such as classes, templates, and exceptions) is more efficient than a shorter alternative (e.g., using standard-library facilities). Often (but of course not always), the opposite is true.

14.3.2.2 void∗

In C, a **void**∗ may be used as the right-hand operand of an assignment to or initialization of a variable of any pointer type; in C++ it may not. For example:

```
void f(int n)
{
    int* p = malloc(n*sizeof(int)); /* not C++; in C++, allocate using "new" */
    // ...
}
```

This is probably the single most difficult incompatibility to deal with. Note that the implicit conversion of a **void**∗ to a different pointer type is *not* in general harmless:

```
char ch;
void* pv = &ch;
int* pi = pv;          // not C++
*pi = 666;             // overwrite ch and other bytes near ch
```

If you use both languages, cast the result of **malloc()** to the right type. If you use only C++, avoid **malloc()**.

14.3.2.3 C++ Keywords

C++ provides many more keywords than C does. If one of these appears as an identifier in a C program, that program must be modified to make it a C++ program:

C++ Keywords That Are Not C Keywords					
alignas	alignof	and	and_eq	asm	bitand
bitor	bool	catch	char16_t	char32_t	class
compl	const_cast	constexpr	decltype	delete	dynamic_cast
explicit	false	friend	inline	mutable	namespace
new	noexcept	not	not_eq	nullptr	operator
or_eq	private	protected	public	reinterpret_cast	static_assert
static_cast	template	this	thread_local	throw	true
try	typeid	typename	using	virtual	wchar_t
xor	xor_eq				

In addition, the word **export** is reserved for future use. C99 adopted **inline**.

In C, some of the C++ keywords are macros defined in standard headers:

C++ Keywords That Are C Macros							
and	and_eq	bitand	bitor	bool	compl	false	not	not_eq
or	or_eq	true	wchar_t	xor	xor_eq		

This implies that in C they can be tested using **#ifdef**, redefined, etc.

14.3.2.4 Linkage

C and C++ can (and often are) implemented to use different linkage conventions. The most basic reason for that is C++'s greater emphasis on type checking. A practical reason is that C++ supports overloading, so that there can be two global functions called **open()**. This has to be reflected in the way the linker works.

To give a C++ function C linkage (so that it can be called from a C program fragment) or to allow a C function to be called from a C++ program fragment, declare it **extern "C"**. For example:

extern "C" double sqrt(double);

Now **sqrt(double)** can be called from a C or a C++ code fragment. The definition of **sqrt(double)** can also be compiled as a C function or as a C++ function.

Only one function of a given name in a scope can have C linkage (because C doesn't allow function overloading). A linkage specification does not affect type checking, so the C++ rules for function calls and argument checking still apply to a function declared **extern"C"**.

14.4   Bibliography

[C,1990]   X3 Secretariat: *Standard – The C Language.* X3J11/90-013. ISO Standard
                            ISO/IEC 9899-1990. Computer and Business Equipment Manufacturers
                            Association. Washington, DC.

[C,1999]   ISO/IEC 9899. *Standard – The C Language.* X3J11/90-013-1999.

[C,2011]   ISO/IEC 9899. *Standard – The C Language.* X3J11/90-013-2011.

[C++,1998]   ISO/IEC JTC1/SC22/WG21 (editor: Andrew Koenig): *International Stan-
                            dard – The C++ Language.* ISO/IEC 14882:1998.

[C++,2004]   ISO/IEC JTC1/SC22/WG21 (editor: Lois Goldtwaite): *Technical Report on
                            C++ Performance.* ISO/IEC TR 18015:2004(E)

[C++Math,2010]   *International Standard – Extensions to the C++ Library to Support Mathe-
                            matical Special Functions.* ISO/IEC 29124:2010.

[C++,2011]   ISO/IEC JTC1/SC22/WG21 (editor: Pete Becker): *International Standard –
                            The C++ Language.* ISO/IEC 14882:2011.

[Cox,2007]   Russ Cox: *Regular Expression Matching Can Be Simple And Fast.* January
                            2007. swtch.com/˜rsc/regexp/regexp1.html.

[Dahl,1970]   O-J. Dahl, B. Myrhaug, and K. Nygaard: *SIMULA Common Base Language.*
                            Norwegian Computing Center S-22. Oslo, Norway. 1970.

[Dechev,2010]   D. Dechev, P. Pirkelbauer, and B. Stroustrup: *Understanding and Effectively
                            Preventing the ABA Problem in Descriptor-based Lock-free Designs.* 13th
                            IEEE Computer Society ISORC 2010 Symposium. May 2010.

[DosReis,2006]   Gabriel Dos Reis and Bjarne Stroustrup: *Specifying C++ Concepts.*
                            POPL06. January 2006.

[Ellis,1989]   Margaret A. Ellis and Bjarne Stroustrup: *The Annotated C++ Reference
                            Manual.* Addison-Wesley. Reading, Mass. 1990. ISBN 0-201-51459-1.

[Friedl,1997]:   Jeffrey E. F. Friedl: *Mastering Regular Expressions.* O'Reilly Media.
                            Sebastopol, California. 1997. ISBN 978-1565922570.

[Gregor,2006]   Douglas Gregor et al.: *Concepts: Linguistic Support for Generic Programming in C++*. OOPSLA'06.

[Ichbiah,1979]   Jean D. Ichbiah et al.: *Rationale for the Design of the ADA Programming Language*. SIGPLAN Notices. Vol. 14, No. 6. June 1979.

[Kernighan,1978] Brian W. Kernighan and Dennis M. Ritchie: *The C Programming Language*. Prentice Hall. Englewood Cliffs, New Jersey. 1978.

[Kernighan,1988] Brian W. Kernighan and Dennis M. Ritchie: *The C Programming Language, Second Edition*. Prentice-Hall. Englewood Cliffs, New Jersey. 1988. ISBN 0-13-110362-8.

[Knuth,1968]   Donald E. Knuth: *The Art of Computer Programming*. Addison-Wesley. Reading, Massachusetts. 1968.

[Koenig,1990]   A. R. Koenig and B. Stroustrup: *Exception Handling for C++ (revised)*. Proc USENIX C++ Conference. April 1990.

[Maddock,2009]   John Maddock: *Boost.Regex*. www.boost.org. 2009.

[Orwell,1949]   George Orwell: *1984*. Secker and Warburg. London. 1949.

[Paulson,1996]   Larry C. Paulson: *ML for the Working Programmer*. Cambridge University Press. Cambridge. 1996. ISBN 0-521-56543-X.

[Richards,1980]   Martin Richards and Colin Whitby-Strevens: *BCPL – The Language and Its Compiler*. Cambridge University Press. Cambridge. 1980. ISBN 0-521-21965-5.

[Stepanov,1994]   Alexander Stepanov and Meng Lee: *The Standard Template Library*. HP Labs Technical Report HPL-94-34 (R. 1). 1994.

[Stroustrup,1982] B. Stroustrup: *Classes: An Abstract Data Type Facility for the C Language*. Sigplan Notices. January 1982. The first public description of "C with Classes."

[Stroustrup,1984] B. Stroustrup: *Operator Overloading in C++*. Proc. IFIP WG2.4 Conference on System Implementation Languages: Experience & Assessment. September 1984.

[Stroustrup,1985] B. Stroustrup: *An Extensible I/O Facility for C++*. Proc. Summer 1985 USENIX Conference.

[Stroustrup,1986] B. Stroustrup: *The C++ Programming Language*. Addison-Wesley. Reading, Massachusetts. 1986. ISBN 0-201-12078-X.

[Stroustrup,1987] B. Stroustrup: *Multiple Inheritance for C++*. Proc. EUUG Spring Conference. May 1987.

[Stroustrup,1987b] B. Stroustrup and J. Shopiro: *A Set of C Classes for Co-Routine Style Programming*. Proc. USENIX C++ Conference. Santa Fe, New Mexico. November 1987.

[Stroustrup,1988] B. Stroustrup: *Parameterized Types for C++*. Proc. USENIX C++ Conference, Denver. 1988.

[Stroustrup,1991] B. Stroustrup: *The C++ Programming Language (Second Edition)*. Addison-Wesley. Reading, Massachusetts. 1991. ISBN 0-201-53992-6.

[Stroustrup,1993] B. Stroustrup: *A History of C++: 1979-1991*. Proc. ACM History of Programming Languages conference (HOPL-2). ACM Sigplan Notices. Vol 28, No 3. 1993.

[Stroustrup,1994]   B. Stroustrup: *The Design and Evolution of C++*. Addison-Wesley. Reading, Mass. 1994. ISBN 0-201-54330-3.

[Stroustrup,1997]   B. Stroustrup: *The C++ Programming Language, Third Edition*. Addison-Wesley. Reading, Massachusetts. 1997. ISBN 0-201-88954-4. Hardcover ("Special") Edition. 2000. ISBN 0-201-70073-5.

[Stroustrup,2002]   B. Stroustrup: *C and C++: Siblings, C and C++: A Case for Compatibility*, and *C and C++: Case Studies in Compatibility*. The C/C++ Users Journal. July-September 2002. www.stroustrup.com/papers.html.

[Stroustrup,2007]   B. Stroustrup: *Evolving a language in and for the real world: C++ 1991-2006*. ACM HOPL-III. June 2007.

[Stroustrup,2009]   B. Stroustrup: *Programming – Principles and Practice Using C++*. Addison-Wesley. 2009. ISBN 0-321-54372-6.

[Stroustrup,2010]   B. Stroustrup: *The C++11 FAQ*. www.stroustrup.com/C++11FAQ.html.

[Stroustrup,2012a]   B. Stroustrup and A. Sutton: *A Concept Design for the STL*. WG21 Technical Report N3351==12-0041. January 2012.

[Stroustrup,2012b]   B. Stroustrup: *Software Development for Infrastructure*. Computer. January 2012. doi:10.1109/MC.2011.353.

[Stroustrup,2013]   B. Stroustrup: *The C++ Programming Language (Fourth Edition)*. Addison-Wesley. 2013. ISBN 0-321-56384-0.

[Sutton,2011]   A. Sutton and B. Stroustrup: *Design of Concept Libraries for C++*. Proc. SLE 2011 (International Conference on Software Language Engineering). July 2011.

[WG21]   ISO SC22/WG21 The C++ Programming Language Standards Committee: *Document Archive*. www.open-std.org/jtc1/sc22/wg21.

[Williams,2012]   Anthony Williams: *C++ Concurrency in Action – Practical Multithreading*. Manning Publications Co. ISBN 978-1933988771.

[Woodward,1974]   P. M. Woodward and S. G. Bond: *Algol 68-R Users Guide*. Her Majesty's Stationery Office. London. 1974.

14.5 Advice

[1]   The material in this chapter roughly corresponds to what is described in much greater detail in Chapters 1 and 44 of [Stroustrup,2013].

[2]   The ISO C++ standard [C++,2011] defines C++.

[3]   When learning C++, don't focus on language features in isolation; §14.2.1.

[4]   By now, many people have been using C++ for a decade or two. Many more are using C++ in a single environment and have learned to live with the restrictions imposed by early compilers and first-generation libraries. Often, what an experienced C++ programmer has failed to notice over the years is not the introduction of new features as such, but rather the changes in relationships between features that make fundamental new programming techniques feasible. In other words, what you didn't think of when first learning C++ or found impractical just might be a superior approach today. You find out only by reexamining the basics. Take the opportunity offered by the new C++11 facilities to modernize your design and

programming techniques:

[1]   Use constructors to establish invariants (§3.4.2).

[2]   Use constructor/destructor pairs to simplify resource management (RAII; §4.2.2).

[3]   Avoid "naked" new and delete (§4.2.2).

[4]   Use containers and algorithms rather than built-in arrays and ad hoc code (Chapter 9, Chapter 10).

[5]   Prefer standard-library facilities to locally developed code (Chapter 6).

[6]   Use exceptions, rather than error codes, to report errors that cannot be handled locally (§3.4).

[7]   Use move semantics to avoid copying large objects (§4.6).

[8]   Use unique_ptr to reference objects of polymorphic type (§11.2.1).

[9]   Use shared_ptr to reference shared objects, that is, objects without a single owner that is responsible for their destruction (§11.2.1).

[10]   Use templates to maintain static type safety (eliminate casts) and avoid unnecessary use of class hierarchies (Chapter 5).

[5]   Before using a new feature in production code, try it out by writing small programs to test the standards conformance and performance of the implementations you plan to use.

[6]   For learning C++, use the most up-to-date and complete implementation of Standard C++ that you can get access to.

[7]   The common subset of C and C++ is not the best initial subset of C++ to learn; §14.3.2.1.

[8]   Prefer named casts, such as static_cast over C-style casts; §14.2.3.

[9]   When converting a C program to C++, first make sure that function declarations (prototypes) and standard headers are used consistently; §14.3.2.

[10]   When converting a C program to C++, rename variables that are C++ keywords; §14.3.2.3.

[11]   For portability and type safety, if you must use C, write in the common subset of C and C++; §14.3.2.1.

[12]   When converting a C program to C++, cast the result of malloc() to the proper type or change all uses of malloc() to uses of new; §14.3.2.2.

[13]   When converting from malloc() and free() to new and delete, consider using vector, push_back(), and reserve() instead of realloc(); §14.3.2.1.

[14]   In C++, there are no implicit conversions from ints to enumerations; use explicit type conversion where necessary.

[15]   Use <string> to get std::string (<string.h> holds the C-style string functions).

[16]   For each standard C header <X.h> that places names in the global namespace, the header <cX> places the names in namespace std.

[17]   Use extern "C" when declaring C functions; §14.3.2.4.

[18]   Prefer string over C-style strings (direct manipulation of zero-terminated arrays of char).

[19]   Prefer iostreams over stdio.

[20]   Prefer containers (e.g., vector) over built-in arrays.

I

Index

Knowledge is of two kinds.
We know a subject ourselves,
or we know where
we can find information on it.
— Samuel Johnson

Token

!=, not-equal operator   6
", string literal   3
$, regex   79
%
    modulus operator   6
    remainder operator   6
%=, operator   7
&
    address-of operator   10
    reference to   10
&&, rvalue reference   51
(, regex   79
(), call operator   64
(? pattern   82
), regex   79
*
    contents-of operator   10
    multiply operator   6
    pointer to   9
    regex   79
*=, scaling operator   7
*? lazy   80
+

plus operator   6
    regex   79
    string concatenation   75
++, increment operator   7
+=
    operator   7
    string append   76
+? lazy   80
-, minus operator   6
--, decrement operator   7
., regex   79
/, divide operator   6
// comment   2
/=, scaling operator   7
: public   40
<<, output operator   2
<=, less-than-or-equal operator   6
<, less-than operator   6
=
    0   39
    and ==   6
    auto   7
    initializer   6
    string assignment   77
==
    = and   6
    equal operator   6
    string   76

as function body, try   99
    try   28
body, function   2
book for beginner   1
bool   5
break   13

C

C   155
    and C++ compatibility   161
    Classic   162
    difference from   161
    K&R   162
    macro, difference from   165
    programmer   168
    void * assignment, difference from   165
    with Classes   154
    with Classes language features   155
    with Classes standard library   156
C++
    ANSI   157
    compatibility, C and   161
    core language   2
    history   153
    ISO   157
    meaning   155
    programmer   168
    pronunciation   155
    standard, ISO   2
    standard library   2
    standardization   157
    timeline   154
C++03   157
C++0x, C++11   155, 158
C++11
    aims   158
    C++0x   155, 158
    language features   158
    library components   159
C++98   157
    standard library   157
C11   161
C89 and C99   161
C99, C89 and   161
call operator ()   64
callback   128
capacity()   97
capture list   65
carries_dependency   159
cast   39
    deprecated C-style   161
    named   161
catch
    clause   28
    every exception   99

catch(...)   99
ceil()   134
char   5
character sets, multiple   77
chrono   125
<chrono>   73, 125, 146
class   34
    concrete   34
    scope   8
    template   59
class
    abstract   40
    base and derived   40
    hierarchy   42
Classic C   162
C-library header   73
clock timing   146
<cmath>   73, 134
cntrl, regex   81
code complexity, function and   4
comment, //   2
communication, task   147
comparison operator   6
compatibility, C and C++   161
compilation
    model, template   68
    separate   24
compiler   2
compile-time
    computation   128
    evaluation   9
complete encapsulation   52
complex   35, 135
<complex>   73, 134–135
complexity, function and code   4
components, C++11 library   159
computation, compile-time   128
concatenation +, string   75
concept   63
concrete
    class   34
    type   34
concurrency   141
condition, declaration in   47
condition_variable   146
    notify_one()   147
    wait()   146
<condition_variable>   146
const, immutability   8
constant expression   9
const_cast   161
constexpr
    function   9
    immutability   8
const_iterator   112
constructor